Elgar

Simon Mundy.

**KING ALFRED'S COLLEGE
WINCHESTER**
Library: 01962 827306

**To be returned on or before the day
marked below, subject to recall**

Elgar

Simon Mundy.

Omnibus Press

London/New York/Sydney/Cologne

This book is dedicated to John Baird

Cover design and art direction by Pearce Marchbank.
Cover photography by George Taylor, Rembrandt Bros.
Cover styled by Annie Hanson.
Properties by Chloe Henderson, Tony Bingham, Ken Paul, Nansi Hanson, The Lacquer Chest.

Printed in Austria.

© Simon Mundy 1980.
First published by Midas Books in 1980.
This edition published in 1984 by Omnibus Press, a division of Book Sales Limited.

Order No. OP 42498
UK ISBN 0.7119.0263.1
US ISBN 0.89524.203.6

Exclusive Distributors:
Book Sales Limited,
8/9 Frith Street,
London, WIV 5TZ,
England.
Music Sales Pty. Limited,
120 Rothschild Avenue,
Roseberg, NSW 2018,
Australia.
To The Music Trade Only:
Music Sales Limited,
8/9 Frith Street,
London, WIV 5TZ,
England.

Frontispiece:
Elgar's Order of Merit regalia.
1911.

Contents

Acknowledgements

I should like to thank the many people and organisations who have made the publication of this book possible: Raymond Monk, for allowing access to his collection of letters and photographs; Jane Whitton, for taking the modern photographs; Joan Coulson of EMI Records, and Jerrold Northrop Moore. For permission to use sources in their possession I am grateful to the Trustees of the Elgar Foundation and the Elgar Birthplace Trust, Mary Evans Picture Library, The Radio Times Hulton Picture Library, Dr. Percy M. Young, Isabella Wallich, Mrs. I.M. Fresson, Novello & Company Ltd., Boosey & Hawkes Ltd., Victor Gollancz Ltd., Hutchinson Publishing Group Ltd., Faber and Faber Ltd., Macdonald & Jane's Ltd., (for the quotation from 'Unfinished Journey' by Yehudi Menuhin), Methuen & Co. Ltd. (for the extract from 'memories of a Variation' by Mrs Richard Powell), Hamish Hamilton Ltd., and Longman Group Ltd.

S.M.

1 Boyhood and Local Musician

A reader of The Times on June 3rd 1857 would have concluded
that the previous day, a Tuesday, had been uninteresting. Glad-
stone had spoken to the Oxford Diocesan Spiritual Help Society
on the benefits of the parochial system; calm had been all but
restored after civil disorder in Belgium and the long controversy
over Mrs. Gaskell's 'Life of Charlotte Brontë' continued in the
letters column. In fact the main news of interest for Englishmen
on June 2nd was not destined to be recognised as such for over
forty years. In 'The Firs', a cottage in the tiny village of
Broadheath, three miles north-west of Worcester, Anne Elgar
gave birth to her second son, Edward William.

Anne's husband, William Henry, had originally come from
Dover but had settled in Worcester in 1841, at the age of nineteen,
as a musician and piano tuner. Although not an exceptional
businessman he had not done badly. In 1844 he was appointed
piano-tuner to Queen Adelaide (the widow of William IV) who
had recently come to live at nearby Witley Court. The piano
dealers, Coventry and Hollier, of Dean Street in London, where
he had served his apprenticeship, had recommended him to the
Comptroller of the Queen Dowager's Household and the position
allowed him to display a Royal Warrant on his stationery. He made
the most of the distinction, riding to the homes of the gentry who
engaged him, whether as violinist, pianist or tuner, on a
thoroughbred horse. Two years later he was appointed organist to
St. George's Roman Catholic Church in Sansome Street. He was
not a Catholic, unlike his wife who was converted from Protestant-
ism, and his interest in the proceedings seems to have been purely
professional. There is a story that before Mass he would hand
round his snuff, damn the organ-blower, and slip across to the
'Hop Market' for refreshment during the sermon. However, the
post was worth £40 per annum and he remained there for thirty-
seven years.

Elgar's birthplace at Broadheath, three miles outside Worcester; now the Elgar Birthplace Museum.

In 1848 he married Anne Greening. She had come from the village of Weston-under-Penyard in the adjacent county of Herefordshire but had moved to Worcester to live with her brother at Claines, just outside the city, and worked in the town centre at the Shades Tavern. William Elgar was the lodger. Anne was a considerably more remarkable woman than this humble sketch suggests. She was well read, being particularly fond of Longfellow (a taste Edward was to inherit) and wrote competent verse all her life. She drew, collected wild flowers and followed current affairs, both local and national, with a clear and inquiring mind. Until 1856 the couple lived in Worcester College Precincts but then, needing by this time more space for their children (Harry was born in 1850, Lucy in 1852 and Polly in 1855), they moved out to Broadheath.

Edward was in fact the only one of their seven children to be born outside the city for, by the time he was three, business forced his father back into the town. By then he had established a shop selling instruments and music, and had taken his younger brother Henry into partnership with him. By 1863 the family had moved once more to the two floors above the Elgar Bros. showroom and shop at 10 High Street (now, sadly, engulfed by a modern shopping development). The other Elgar children (Joe, Frank and

The baby Edward Elgar with his mother in a daguerreotype picture of 1859.

Worcester Cathedral from across the River Severn in the middle of the nineteenth century.

Helen) were all born in the town, though Harry and Joe (who was Edward's closest companion and was considered the musical prodigy of the family) both died in childhood. There can have been few families of any size in nineteenth century England that survived into adulthood intact.

Worcester in the middle of the century was a thriving city, more prosperous than most West Country towns, near enough to the Midland centres of industry to benefit (especially its pottery), but still a focal point for rural life. Although the ancient cloth industry was in decline, hops and fruit were traded extensively and the city boasted three markets a week: on Wednesdays, Fridays and Saturdays. The river Severn was navigable for vessels of up to eighty tons while the Worcester-Birmingham canal linked (and still does) the river to the fast-growing factories of the 'Black Country'. But apart from its trade and prosperity this Cathedral city was one of the most beautiful in the country. The Cathedral was founded in 680 A.D. by Ethelred, King of Mercia, and rebuilt in 1084 by St. Wulstan, the only Saxon bishop to keep his See after the Norman Invasion. In his will of 1216 King John asked to be buried in front of the altar between the shrines of St. Wulstan and St. Oswald and three hundred years later the young Prince Arthur, elder brother of King Henry VIII, was brought from Ludlow after his death and laid in the elaborate chantry chapel nearby. Concomitant with its position as a major See were the college (originally founded in 1541 with provision for forty King's scholars), cloisters and Bishop's palace. 'To the south of the Cathedral is an open space called the college Green', reported a county guide in about 1840, 'a little to the west of which is the site of the ancient castle, which was formerly a large and magnificent structure, of which, however, but few traces at present remain and those little indicative of its pristine importance. Edgar's Tower, which still braves the assaults of time, constituted the principal entrance to the castle and is the finest remnant of antiquity in the whole city . . . This city possesses the singular advantage of having a number of highly agreeable walks in its vicinity, all of which abound in picturesque scenery . . . The Foregate Street being broad, well-paved and airy, is resorted to as a fashionable promenade. During the summer months the gardens on the west side of the Severn answer the same purpose.'

The countryside, dominated by Worcestershire Beacon, rising 1400ft. above the valley, was as rich in history. Caractacus, the great British chieftain, had been pursued by the Romans to the Malvern Hills where he was finally captured and the last great battle of the Civil War was fought there. To a boy as aware of topography, landscape and history as Edward proved to be, it was an immensely rich heritage that caught his imagination as a child and never allowed him to feel at home anywhere else, however suffocating he found its provinciality and narrow prejudices. Culturally Worcester was better endowed than many similar places, the focal point being the Three Choirs Festival, held jointly with Gloucester and Hereford and, founded in 1724, the oldest music festival in Britain. Aside from the Festival's triennial sojourn at Worcester, the city supported a good plurality of music societies; the Glee Club, the Harmonic Society, the Instrumental Society and the Madrigal Society, in all of which the Elgar family were active, and which were to give the young Edward some of his first opportunities both as a player and as a composer.

William Elgar, although he was not ambitious for his children (in fact he at first tried to discourage Edward from becoming a professional musician – probably as a result of his own awareness of the financial insecurity it involved) was determined that they should all have at least a rudimentary knowledge of music and so Edward took up the piano, violin and organ; Frank, the oboe, and Polly learned to sing, an accomplishment fitting and expected of young ladies. Edward's first piano lessons were given when he went to a 'dame school' in Britannia Place and later he had violin lessons from Frederick Spray, leader of the Worcester Glee Club Orchestra and a respected local musician. His proper schooling, however, took place at Littleton House, an establishment of about

The Elgar children in 1868. L. to R. (standing): Polly, Lucy; (seated): Helen (Dot), Edward, Frank.

thirty pupils run by Francis Reeve, a teacher destined to have his own place in the Elgar mythology.

Edward was a nervous, dreamy child. His friend Hubert Leicester, later Mayor of Worcester, remembered:–

He was a miserable looking lad – legs like drumsticks – nothing of a boy about him. One great characteristic, though, always doing *something*. When he stopped away from school, which he did about a third of the time, it was not merely to play truant.

Elgar himself thought of those days with affection when he wrote a preface to Leicester's book *Forgotten Worcester* sixty years later:-

Before starting [for school] our finances were rigidly inspected . . . the report being favourable, two pence were allowed for the ferry. Descending the steps, past the door behind which the mythical salmon is incised, we embarked: at our backs 'the unthrift sun shot vital gold', filling Payne's Meadows and illuminating for two small boys a world to conquer and to love.

Edward was a talented though not particularly precocious boy. Nevertheless, when he was eleven, and the Elgar children wanted to put on a play, they looked to him for the music. The imaginary scene was a 'woodland glade' across a stream which effectively barred adults and other unnecessary evils of the real world.

'Our orchestral means were meagre', he wrote later, 'a piano forte, two or three strings, a flute and some improvised percussion were all we could depend upon; the double-bass was of our own manufacture and three pounds of nails went into its making . . . [and] consisted wholly of three notes (A,D,G), the open strings of the (old English) double-bass. The usual player (myself) was wanted for stage management, but the simplicity . . . made it possible for a child who knew nothing of music to grind out the bass.'

Simple the tunes may have been, but he kept the sketches and often revised them. Forty years later they were reworked as the *Wand of Youth Suites*. It was about the same time, in 1869, that he decided that the violin, rather than the piano, most interested him. He had heard the aria *O thou that tellest* from Handel's *Messiah* sung in the Cathedral and went home determined to teach himself to play it.

In one thing he was exceptional – his ability to read and understand printed music from an early age, without recourse to the sound. It was this ability, his developed 'inner ear', that made it possible for him to achieve a high degree of theoretical proficiency

The old High Street, Worcester. Elgar Brothers' shop is in front of the man with the bicycle.

with a minimum of formal tuition. Indeed it was this independence from academic constraint, the fact that he was self-taught, in a way that none of his contemporaries were, burrowing away in the fusty atmosphere of the London colleges, that made his music individual and idiomatic from the first. He was, of course, surrounded by music in his father's shop, but if he wanted his own copy of a score to study and note it was as expensive a business for him as for any other boy. When he did acquire a score it was immediately devoured.

The first which came into my hands were the Beethoven Symphonies . . . and I remember the day I was able to buy the *Pastoral Symphony*. I stuffed my pockets with bread and cheese and went out into the fields to study it. That is what I always did.

When he left school in 1872 at the age of fifteen, he was, like most lower middle-class boys, expected to start fending for himself. There was no thought of him turning into a musician, at least not for the moment. Instead he was taken on by a local lawyer, William Allen, a friend of the family through his membership of the St. George's congregation. As with everything he did, Edward applied himself to the law with seriousness. However, he was soon to find that the duties of the office boy were more likely to involve washing the floors than training for the bar. He did learn a certain amount about book-keeping so that when he finally decided, after a year's legal drudgery, that the profession was definitely not for him, he was able to offer tangible qualifications to his father (whose accounting procedures seem to have left much to be desired) when he started at Elgar Bros. as an assistant. Two events during the previous year had made the move more sensible. In

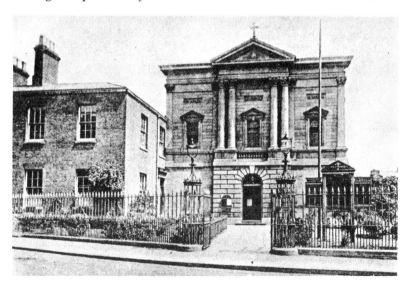

St. George's, Sansome St., Worcester, where the Elgars (father and son) were both organist.

July 1872 he had deputised for his father for the first time at mass in the organ loft of St. George's; and in January he had appeared as a violinist, with other local players, at a concert given in the Union Workhouse; not perhaps the most exalted of venues to begin a career, but a professional engagement nonetheless.

Once the decision to become a musician was made, Elgar, although an accomplished all-round player for his age, resolved to study the subject properly. Amongst the books in the shop, where he now had unrestricted access and time for browsing, were the classic texts he needed to give himself a grounding in harmony and counterpoint. He read Cherubini's *Counterpoint*, Catel's *Treatise on Harmony* and Berlioz' *Instrumentation* but the work he found most helpful was Novello's translation (1854) of *Mozart's Succinct Thorough-Bass School*. As he later remarked to George Bernard Shaw, 'the only document in existence of the smallest use to the student composer.' He found in it 'something to go upon – something human'.

Having successfully made his début at St. George's, Edward found himself called upon to accompany the services more frequently, which no doubt allowed his father extended contemplation in the 'Hop Market'. But, since the Catholic services were over sooner than those at the Cathedral, he often would rush from one end of the High Street to the other to hear the final voluntary played on the magnificent new organ. He was unlikely to hear anything revolutionary at that time for the organist, William Done, also conductor of the Worcester Festival Choral Society, was an implacable conservative who, though a staunch champion of Tallis, Gibbons, Corelli and Purcell, regarded Schumann and all that followed him with the deepest suspicion as 'modernists'. However, if the romantics were not allowed to infiltrate the Cathedral precincts, there was an occasional chance to hear operas by Verdi and Bellini as mounted by the Haig-Dyer Opera Company, one of that persevering chain of ensembles that toured the provinces with small means and reduced bands playing, as Basil Maine put it, 'for the sake of the five and twenty just men that were found in each of the towns of their itinerary'. The performances might not have been up to the standards of La Scala, but with a little imagination and a seat far enough away from the stage make-up and tatty scenery, the possible effect could be guessed.

But the young Elgar was foremost a performing, rather than a listening, lover of music. Apart from his duties in church he soon joined the ranks of the Worcester Glee Club, for which his father had been a violinist and occasional accompanist since about 1843, and whose meetings took place with much smoking and drinking at the tables of the Crown Hotel. The Glee Club, in its small but encouraging way, proved to be a generous patron. The music that was played was again conservative: mainly overtures by Handel, Balfe and Rossini and symphonies by Haydn. But they were prepared to hear whatever local talent (not only Elgar) presented to them and gave valuable experience, whether as arranger, composer or violinist.

Sunday afternoon was also a time for music making. A wind quintet was formed consisting of Frank Exton and Hubert Leicester (flutes), Frank Elgar (oboe), William Leicester (clarinet) and

The wind quintet for the Sunday afternoon 'potting shed' gatherings. Standing L. to R. William Leicester, Elgar, Hubert Leicester, (seated) Frank Exton, Frank Elgar.

The only picture of Elgar with his violin, taken in his early twenties.

Edward Elgar (bassoon). 'There was no music to suit our peculiar requirements so I used to write the music . . . it was an understood thing that we should have a new piece every week. The sermons in our church used to take at least half an hour, and I spent the time composing the thing for the afternoon', he said in an interview of 1904. The rehearsals took place in the potting shed and the music was a good deal more sophisticated than their concert hall! For nearly a hundred years the pieces were 'lost' to performance. Recently, however, the parts for these endearing and relaxed works were found. The first public performance of Elgar's Harmony Music Four (named with reference to the German 'harmoniemusik') and Five Intermezzos was finally given at London's Wigmore Hall in July 1978. These pieces do not deserve to be dismissed as juvenilia, 'worth nothing in themselves', for even if they do not reflect the intensity of the later Elgar, they show a high degree of craftmanship and have an energy and humour all their own. Above all they show that at twenty-one, in 1878, Elgar had mastered the surety and confidence of instrumental effect that was later to be his greatest hallmark. There are, to my mind, few collections of music for the medium that show as much understanding of the form or give as much pleasure to the listener, light as they are.

He had always hoped to be able to go to Leipzig to study, and had started to save up the money for the trip, but it proved to be beyond his means. However, there was enough (£7. 15s 9d. to be exact) to go to London for a twelve day visit. The real purpose was a series of five lessons with Adolf Pollitzer, the leader of the Philharmonic Society Orchestra and the Royal Choral Society, (considerably more of a force in the musical life of the capital then than it is now), as well as the Opera Orchestra at Covent Garden. These lessons – which disposed of nearly half the savings straight away – were to prove a sound investment, for Pollitzer not only suggested, in vain as it turned out, that the young violinist return for further more regular lessons, he also interceded with August Manns for Elgar's compositions in the following years. Pollitzer was encouraging to his pupil perhaps because he himself, when aged thirteen, had been helped by Mendelssohn after playing through part of the *Violin Concerto*. However, Elgar decided that he did not want to follow the life of a virtuoso player mainly, he said, because he did not feel his tone was full enough. His second reason for going to London was the chance to hear the concerts put on by Manns at the Crystal Palace, built originally for the Great Exhibition of 1851. It is difficult for us now, when there is a plethora of concert halls and five world class symphony orchestras in London alone, to realise what an innovatory figure Manns was for, from 1855 until 1901, he conducted programmes every day, with a major event every Saturday afternoon. Although he had first arrived in England from Germany as a military bandsman, he was responsible for introducing the music of Brahms, Wagner and Schubert. He also gave the first London performance of Elgar's music and was the young composer's sole contact, as he was for thousands of others, with well-played European modern music. After his first visit Elgar went up to London as often as he could, and eventually Manns gave him a rehearsal pass:

I lived 120 miles from London. I rose at six, walked a mile to the railway station, the train left at seven; arrived at Paddington about eleven, underground to Victoria, on to the Palace arriving in time for the last three-quarters of an hour of rehearsal; if fortune smiled, this . . . included the work desired to be heard; but fortune rarely smiled and more often than not the principal item was over. Lunch. Concert at three. At five a rush to Victoria; then to Paddington, on to Worcester arriving at 10.30. A strenuous day indeed; but the new work had been heard . . .'.

At home in Worcester he continued his study of the great masters. On one occasion he set himself the task of writing a symphony, taking Mozart's G minor symphony as his model, ruling the same number of bars and using the same instruments. 'I did this on my own initiative,' he told a reporter from The Strand Magazine in 1904, 'as I was groping in the dark after light, but looking back over 30 years I don't know any discipline from which I learned so much.' He also arranged pieces for use at St. George's, and there he found a ready outlet for his own music for use in the services and the festivals of the church calendar. In 1879 the church celebrated its fiftieth anniversary and Elgar obliged with two liturgical settings, *Domine Salvum Fac* and *Tantum Ergo*. A year later he contributed a *Salve Regina* to a service marking the opening of a new chancel; his father played the organ while he led the orchestra. He had also written an Easter anthem, *Brother for Thee who died*, and two hymn tunes, one of which was published in the Westminster hymnal. In 1877 he had been an early member, 'leader and instructor' of the Worcester Amateur Instrumental Society who made him their conductor two years later. He was becoming a local musical general factotum in the same way that his father had done at the same age; useful and occupied, though not well paid, a stalwart in the cultural life of the county, able to knock the odd tune or anthem together when they were required.

One of the more bizarre appointments he accepted was the post of Bandmaster to the Attendant's Orchestra at Worcestershire County Lunatic Asylum at Powick, where the doctors evidently had a remarkably advanced idea of the value of music therapy. The duties, as well as conducting, included the arranging and writing of music for the band, each new piece earning him an extra 5/- on top of the £32 a year of his salary. His orchestra, for which Quadrilles were the favourite form (although the odd polka or lancer went down as well), was almost as fragmentary as that scratched together for his childhood plays. There were piccolo, flute, clarinet, euphonium, bombardon and two cornets; the strings consisting of between six and eight violins, a viola once in a while, a 'cello and bass. However the stream of music did give him a chance to dedicate a set of five quadrilles called *Die Junge Kokette* to Miss Holloway, the staff pianist. Another set, entitled *Paris*, were penned in the same direction. In later years the composer enjoyed deflating sycophantic admirers by beginning a conversation, 'When I was at the Lunatic Asylum' . . . '

Paris stemmed from his first visit abroad, to France in 1880, with Charles Pipe, a merchant soon to become his brother-in-law when he married Lucy. While there he heard Saint-Saëns play the organ at La Madeleine and went to the theatre to see some Molière. His mind was not, it seems, continually on Miss Holloway, however, as somebody had stimulated a brief romance at Barbizon.

On his return he was promoted to the first violins in the Worcester Festival Orchestra. Earlier that year (1881) his piece *Air de Ballet* had been played by Worcester Amateur Instrumental Society and it was repeated when the orchestra played for a concert in celebration of the British Medical Association's Jubilee meeting in August 1882. At the conference was a young doctor, Charles Buck, six years older than Elgar, whose practice was at Settle in Yorkshire. Buck was an accomplished amateur musician and the two became firm friends. Elgar was a prolific and excellent letter-writer. His style was conversational and easy with close friends, like Buck (with whom he corresponded for the rest of his life) and later, August Jaeger. He used the letter to express and, one suspects, purge himself of the deeply-felt moods of depression and dejection that were not only an intrinsic part of his character, but also seem to have been a major force behind his drive to compose. The feelings of rejection and often rather self-indulgent helplessness grew rather than diminished with his fame. Throughout his life he used to reiterate the cry that nobody understood or wanted his music, which for much of the time was patently untrue. Composing, though, is an exhausting mental process and Elgar undoubtedly used his friends to share the emotional strain that was an inevitable part of his work.

However, his letters are by no means all despondency and gloom; frequently they are full of acute observation and an exuberant sense of fun, as in the stories he sent back to Buck about the puppy the doctor had given him in 1885:-

12

This morning I had let him out at 7.30 into the river and he had his first fight with a Newfoundland brute which began it; no harm done . . . The Bath road presents a perfect paradise of new smells all of which he has duly examined and *'reported'* on.

Later he wrote;

I shut him up at the shop this morn: while I went to give a lesson, he whined so his grandmother let him out, he darted down the stairs, caught his leg in twenty concertinas that are piled on the staircase and rolled over with all the lot into the middle of the shop! There were some ladies there and my old father enjoyed it awfully.

At the end of 1882 Elgar achieved his ambition to visit Leipzig. There was still not enough money to allow him to stay and study for any length of time, but the trip did give him a chance to sample the more cosmopolitan concert-giving of the Continent, in the form of the Leipzig Gewandhaus Orchestra, once conducted by Mendelssohn but for the last twenty years by the great Carl Reinecke. His arrival in Leipzig on New Year's Eve started a little disconcertingly, as R.J. Buckley recounted in his biography of 1904:-

On the stroke of midnight Elgar entered a hotel where a waiter, mistaking him for a new year guest, ushered the astonished traveller into the thick of a private party standing on chairs, wearing paper caps of wonderful shapes and colours, and at that precise moment raising their glasses with shouts of 'Prosit Neu-jahr!' Among the throng of revellers Elgar, with his travelling-cap, overcoat and umbrella . . . bowed and fled . . .

Apart from wanting to sample the high standard of the Opera and the Gewandhaus Orchestra, Elgar eagerly looked forward to hearing music by Schumann and Wagner, at that time, following the lead of 'authorities' like the Worcester organist William Done, considered unworthy in provincial England. At the concerts in January he heard Schumann's *Piano Concerto* and the *Overture, Scherzo and Finale* which he enjoyed, although he found it lightweight. 'The opening reminds me of Cherubini's overture to *The Water-carrier*, not thematically, but in the pattern.' He also heard the Prelude to *Parsifal* and Anton Rubinstein's *Ocean Symphony*. He soaked himself in as much music as he could find, some of it familiar:-

We used to attend the rehearsals at the Gewandhaus; 9 a.m.! Most of our pros. are not up by that time . . . The first thing I heard was Haydn Sym. in G – the Surprise. Fancy!! I was so astounded. I thought it strange to go so far to hear so little. After that I got pretty well dosed with Schumann (my ideal!), Brahms, Rubinstein and Wagner, so had no cause to complain.

The Neuen Gewandhaus, Leipzig. In 1882 Elgar achieved his ambition to visit Leipzig, and though he couldn't afford to study, he did attend concerts and rehearsals.

Elgar very satisfactorily combined business with pleasure by including a young English girl called Edith on his visits to the opera, but he was also interested (it appears rather more so) in a German girl who was a student in Leipzig and who visited him for most of that summer in Worcester. He wrote to Buck on July 1st.

The vacation at Leipzig begins shortly; my "Braut" arrives here on Thursday next remaining till the first week of September; of course I shall remain in Worcester till her departure. After that 'twould be a charity if you could find a broken-hearted fiddler much trio-playing for a day or two.

That, intriguingly, is the last we hear of her. However Elgar, in this at least, was a very normal man and was never against a spot of flirtation. The following year's holiday in Scotland saw another brief romance which came to nothing. He was always attractive to women; tall, handsome and lean, from his early twenties sporting a fashionable and characteristically luxuriant moustache. His volatile moods (one moment enthusiastic and excited, the next fierce, and dreamy at another) combined with his ambitions as a composer (in themselves romantic) caught the imagination and, as we shall see later, brought out a streak of possessiveness in women.

By the autumn of 1883 he had been playing not only for Worcester orchestras but also for the Popular Concerts run by W.C. Stockley in Birmingham. These, apart from the various periodic festivals were the Midlands' major regular concerts and on 13th December the programme included Elgar's *Intermezzo: Sérénade Mauresque*. Stockley recalled the event in a letter of 1900;

Mostines 1st Oct. . . . my first real knowledge of him came from Dr. Herbert Wareing, who told me that Elgar was a clever writer and suggested that I should play one of his compositions at one of my concerts. At my request Wareing brought me a Romance (*sic*) (I think it was) and I at once recognised its merit and offered to play it. This I did and his modesty on the occasion is certainly worth notice, for on my asking him if he would like to conduct he declined, and, further, insisted on playing in his place in the orchestra.

It was an important occasion for the twenty-six year old composer, for it was his first foray outside the immediate neighbourhood of Worcester and the first time he had collected any number of Press comments. One of the more heartening reviews was very fair, if not rapturous:

The High Street, Birmingham in the 1880s.

Judging from the results the director will not regret giving a helping hand to rising talent . . . Mr. Elgar justifies his assumption of a place in the

programme . . . we hasten to give Mr. Elgar every credit for a musicianly work. A unanimous recall served to discover quite a young composer to the audience; and as Mr. Elgar is not deficient in scholarship, has plenty of fancy, and orchestrates with facility, we may hope he will not "rest and be thankful" but go on in a path for which he possesses singular qualifications.

Not the sort of notice to send a novice composer to Heaven, but new works have received considerably worse! In January, a month after the performance, he wrote to Buck (who was soon to be married). The letter is worth quoting at length because it is typical of his reaction after almost every first performance.

I had a good success at Birm. despite what the papers say; the man who wrote the slighting article is a Mus. Bac. who had sent in two pieces and they were advertised and withdrawn because the orchestration wanted so much revision as to be unplayable! Enough of this – I had a characteristic letter from Pollitzer – he asked for the parts and is trying to introduce the sketch in London – I don't anticipate a performance tho' I will let you know if it comes off. I was sorely disappointed at not going to town – but 'tis no use going there to sit in the house all day – well – I have no money – not a cent. And I am sorry to say I have no prospects of getting any. We have had a very quiet time; my father was ill just before Xmas which made it dismal; the younger generation at the Catholic Ch: have taken an objection to him and have got him turned out of the Organist's place; this he had held for 37 years!! He thinks a great deal of this and I fear 'twill break him up. Frank gets on: . . . and it seems to me the only person who is an utter failure in this miserable world is myself . . . I am disappointed, disheartened and sick of this world altogether'. **There was however one alleviating pleasure.** 'P.S. Miss Weaver is remaining in Worcester and the little Music *etc*. that we get together is the only enjoyment I get and more than I deserve no doubt.

Family relations were not improved the following year when he took over the Organist's position at St. George's that his father had had to give up.

Whatever the problems and the lack of money, which was to persist for a good many years to come, 1884 was professionally an excellent period. *Sevilliana*, one of his most charming light works, was given its première under William Done by the Worcester Philharmonic Society on 1st May and eleven days later, thanks to Pollitzer's continued championship of his pupil, it became the first music by Elgar to be heard in London, when Manns conducted it during an exhibition concert at Crystal Palace. But again the emotional strain of the event took its toll, and depressed and exhausted Elgar left to recover in Scotland.

In September, at the Worcester Festival, Elgar was made aware

Antonin Dvorak
(1841-1904). Elgar played
amongst the violins when
Dvorak conducted in
Birmingham.

of his ambitions beyond the confines of English popular concerts
when he came into contact with Dvořák, then cementing his
growing reputation in Britain with his second visit of the year. He
conducted his *Stabat Mater* in the Cathedral, as well as his D major
symphony (now listed as no.6). The fierce eyes, tousled beard and
Bohemian scowl of the forty-three year-old Czech must have
looked refreshingly out of place in the genteel atmosphere of
Worcester – Elgar, playing in his usual place amongst the violins of
the Festival Orchestra, was enthralled by his first close proximity
to a creative musician of world stature (incidentally – another 'self-
taught' composer), and was immediately won over by the music. 'I
wish', he wrote to Buck, 'you could hear Dvořák's music. It is
simply ravishing, so tuneful and clever and the orchestration is
wonderful; no matter how few instruments he uses it never sounds
thin. I cannot describe it; it must be heard.' He had found another
aesthetic model to place with Schumann and Brahms, including
the *Slavonic Dances* in the concerts he conducted as often as
possible. Two years later he played the same symphony again
under Dvořák, this time at Stockley's Birmingham concert.

In the meantime John Beare, Charles Buck's brother-in-law,
published *Une Idylle*, dedicated to Elgar's fancy of 1883, 'Miss
E.E. of Inverness'. Schott's also began taking pieces for publication, in particular the *Romance* for violin and piano of 1878, which
was issued as Opus 1 and dedicated, in a typical display of un-
snobbish friendship, to Oswin Grainger, a local grocer, who
played in the amateur orchestras.

The next few years were neither a period of stagnation, nor of
conspicuous advance. Midlands orchestral societies continued to
include whatever he produced and a selection of songs and
chamber pieces, none aimed at anything other than the drawing-
room market, continued to be published. He wrote more for the
services at St. George's, an *Ave Verum* (1887) and *Ecce Sacerdos
Magnus* (1888). That year he conducted Stockley's orchestra for
the first time in his Suite in D, an amalgam of four pieces including
the *Sérénade Mauresque* and the March *Pas Redoublé*, which he had
written in 1882. The final movement, *Contrasts*, is one of his finest
and most craftsman-like early works. When it was published in
1899 as part of the *Three Characteristic Pieces* he wrote to August
Jaeger of Novello's

I saw two dancers once in Leipzig who came down the stage in antique
dress dancing a gavotte: when they reached the footlights they suddenly
turned round and appeared to be two very young and modern people and
danced a gay and lively measure; they had come down the stage *back-
wards* & danced away with their (modern) faces towards us – when they
reached the back of the stage they suddenly turned round and the old,

decrepit couple danced gingerly to the old tune. I tell you all this because it gave me the idea of the IIIrd. movement of the three things I sent to the firm.'

The press were lukewarm, as he told Buck, 'The critics, save two are nettled. I am the only local man who has been asked to conduct his own work – & what's a greater offence. I *did* it – and *well* too . . .

Elgar was much in demand as a soloist, giving violin recitals for the various clubs, soirées and charitable societies of the neighbourhood at two guineas a time; and he augmented his meagre earnings (having earlier resigned from the lunatic asylum) by teaching a clutch of young, middle-class ladies in Malvern. His favourites were the Gedge sisters, who prompted an Allegretto for violin and piano based on the notes of their name, the Acworths, and Hilda and Isabel Fitton. An older friend of the Fitton family, Caroline Alice Roberts, came to his teaching room in Malvern on October 6th 1886, having seen his advertisement in the paper. After the old coachman had driven her to Malvern for two or three months, he was heard to say that he thought there was more in it than music. Edward gave her an engagement ring on 26th January 1889 and Charles Buck and the groom's parents travelled to London for the marriage at Brompton Oratory at noon on 8th May.

2 Married Teacher: Festival Composer

Marrying Caroline Alice Roberts turned out to be one of the most far-sighted actions Edward ever took, professionally, socially, and, of course, personally. However, like most things in his life, the process was not straightforward. The initial difficulties, which left their scars, brought out several traits of character that, although latent, had previously not been apparent. But the problems were due more to the class and religious prejudices of the Victorian age than to any fault of the couple involved. Though both Alice's parents were dead, her remaining family and many of their friends objected wholeheartedly to her choice of husband on social grounds. Firstly, there was the question of pedigree. Edward's family were tradesmen and, though music was perhaps a shade more respectable than the grocer's trade, it was definitely still on the wrong side of the social fence. Alice's family, however, was of the gentry with a tradition of service in India. Her father, Henry Gee Roberts, had joined the East India Company aged eighteen, in 1818, and was a Major in the Bombay Native Light Infantry by 1835. Alice was born in 1848 and her father was promoted to the rank of Colonel and later Major-General. Three years later (in 1859), having successfully played his part in crushing the Mutiny, he retired and returned home to Hazeldine House in the Gloucestershire village of Redmarley D'Abitot as Sir Henry Gee Roberts, Knight Commander of the Bath. He did not live long to enjoy the house he had bought for his retirement, for he died in 1860. Alice's upbringing was strictly military, with discipline and an absolute code based on unquestioned tradition and precedent governing all aspects of behaviour. Marrying below one's station was not part of it. Fifteen years later the position was reversed, but to the Roberts family at the time Elgar was no more than a local jobbing musician and a penniless one at that.

Then there was the problem of religion. Alice Elgar's maternal grandfather, Robert Raikes, had been in the forefront of the

Edward and Caroline
Alice Elgar just after their
marriage.

movement to create Anglican Sunday Schools. By the time of their marriage Catholicism was tolerated but not condoned. To the Church of England and therefore the establishment mind, 'damned Popery' was objectionable not only on grounds of dogma but, far more important to the Victorians, it implied allegiance on earth to an authority higher than the British Sovereign as Defender of the Faith. Since the constitutional arrangements of the country involve government by the dual body of the King in Parliament (of which the bishops are a part) Catholicism was seen to mean not only a difference of religious detail, but also a partial renunciation of the English State. Indeed, it was not until the Catholic Emancipation Act of 1829 that Catholics were allowed to hold public office at all; the final legal barriers were not removed until the 1870s. The Elgars bore the additional stigma of being converts and therefore did not have the excuse that their religion was an accident of birth, a far more understandable state of affairs. Mixed marriages, of course, found favour with neither church: indeed, their wedding service was given in a shortened version because Alice was, at that time, a Protestant. Now, in an increasingly secular society, such divisions seem irrelevant, but in the 1880s, especially in the complacent middle-class conservatism of the Severn Valley, they aroused real fears and passions.

Finally there was the difference in age. At forty Alice, having dutifully looked after her mother and evaded marriage, would normally have been set for perpetual spinsterhood, and it cannot have escaped the thoughts of her sober-minded relatives that, in accepting a man of inferior class nearly nine years her junior, she was making a rather desperate and imprudent last-minute dash to the altar.

The combined pressures of English snobbery and religious bigotry left an indelible impression on Elgar's character. One part of him attempted to become all the things he was not. He adopted the clothes and stance of the country gentleman, giving himself a military air, perhaps in deference to his wife's background. His speech, when not excited, was measured and deliberate with, as Arnold Bax later noted, a hint of hauteur and reserve. This, as well as being a satisfactory mask for natural shyness, also helped to disguise his Worcestershire accent. Safe behind his defences he contained his feelings though, when the storms broke, as they inevitably did, and the intensity of composition was not adequate release, his temper and depression could be fierce.

Alice's approach was very different. For her marriage to Edward was the final move in the proof of her intellectual independence that had started in work with the amateur geologist the Rev. William Symonds and had found its most complete satisfaction in the publication of her novel *Marchcroft Manor* (1882) and the epic poem *Isobel Trevithoe* (1879). She was by no means the only Victorian spinster to write prose and (it must be said) indifferent poetry, but it was something to have them in print. Collaborating with Elgar on songs and nurturing his genius became to her a duty and full-time occupation that satisfied both her need for artistic expression and her instincts as a late, and therefore even more zealous, wife. When she was younger she had wanted to reform society; if not as actively as her cousin Emily, a charity helper in Paddington. Perhaps in marrying against the conventions of her class she felt that, strengthened by her conviction of Elgar's potential, she had done something to that end.

For the moment though, the couple were cocooned in the business of marriage. The honeymoon was spent at Ventnor on the Isle of Wight, which then enjoyed the fashion fostered by the presence of the Queen's retreat at Osborne.

Ventnor on the Isle of Wight, where the Elgars spent their honeymoon. The proximity of the Queen's house at Osborne made it a highly fashionable watering place.

They were both determined that marriage should herald a new start, leaving behind the drudgery of provincial teaching and, in Alice's case, housecalls with her mother. She had a certain amount of money of her own which made it possible to set up house in London, for a few months, at first in Fountain Road, Upper Norwood in the southern suburbs, usefully near the Crystal Palace and Manns' concerts, to which they had season tickets. Manns continued to be

The Crystal Palace at Sydenham; everything from August Manns' concerts to the dog show.

helpful whenever he could, including the *Suite* (that Stockley had put on in Birmingham) in two programmes in November 1889, repeating it in February 1890. For half-a-crown Edward was able to go to Covent Garden where he could indulge in Wagner as well as the more usual fare of *Carmen* and *Don Giovanni*. At the Lyceum Theatre he saw Verdi's *Otello*, finished two years before, during its first London run conducted by its first conductor, Franco Faccio. At St. James's Hall, Richter held his concerts and there were the great celebrity recitals. Non-musical activities took them to the theatre and art galleries and to the Crystal Palace Dog Show, for Edward was, if anything, rather more fond of dogs than humans.

Determined that his compositions should succeed, Elgar tramped the streets round Piccadilly and Soho, the haunts of publishers, offering his pieces for sale. Many were taken (one wonders, indeed, whether he would have had such success touting unsolicited manuscripts these days); Novello's, after a tussle over copyright, published his partsong *My Love Dwelt in a Northern Land*, with words by Andrew Lang, who at first objected to the setting but was eventually mollified. The odd piece for violin and piano, another song and eleven organ voluntaries (given to Mrs. Vera Raikes, whose house in Norwood they were borrowing and the only one of Alice's relations to be fully behind the marriage) were taken by Osborne and Tuckwood.

Schott's willingly relieved him of *Liebesgruss*, written on a visit to Charles Buck at Settle just before he got engaged to Alice, changed the title to *Salut d'Amour* and published it for piano solo and violin and piano as well as issuing the orchestral parts and a full score. 'Four editions!!', he wrote to Buck, 'gusto!!!'. The piece was helped on its way to popularity by Manns who gave it a performance on November 11th 1889. It sold exceptionally well and Schott's made a considerable amount of money. Elgar, however, had sold it to them outright for about £5. Had he not done so, perhaps the financial problems which were to complicate his life for many years might have been less traumatic. At the time Alice had to sell her pearls to maintain their standards. Both the management of the Covent Garden Promenade Concerts and Frederic Cowen (five years older than Elgar but already Sullivan's successor as conductor of the Philharmonic Society) were encouraging if not enthusiastic enough to mount performances.

Surprisingly it was Worcester, now that Elgar was established in London, that provided the most heartening news, at last commissioning a work for the 1890 Three Choirs Festival. Four years earlier he had written to Buck, 'I have retired into my shell and live in hopes of writing a polka someday – failing that a single chant is probably my fate.' Then the words had seemed too true for comfort: now there seemed the possibility that they would be belied, for the Festivals, strongholds of the musical establishment of which Elgar was so conspicuously not a part, at that time held the key to national popularity, if not international renown.

The winter had been mixed. He suffered from nervous headaches and the eye and throat complaint that often troubled him when the weather was bad and morale low. On the better side, though, they found a house at 51, Avonmore Road, West Kensington which they took on a three year lease and moved into in March. Best of all was the knowledge, early in the new year, that Alice was pregnant.

By May he was at work on the overture for Worcester. The idea, typically Victorian and gothically romantic, stemmed from the historical tales of Froissart epitomised in the line from Keats with which Elgar prefixed the score; 'When chivalry lifted up her lance on high . . .' *Froissart* is really Elgar's first work for full-scale symphony orchestra and it shows his idiomatic touches of orchestration and – for the first time – the grandeur of his symphonic writing. Once the cumbersome 'programme' is forgotten it stands as a remarkably assured piece for a composer who, although the orchestra was to him as natural a medium as breathing, had never attempted anything on that scale before. The criticisms of the time, that it lacked unity, were to an extent justified. Some of the episodes are a little abrupt and the lyrical central section is perhaps too close to the repetitive cosiness of his 'salon' pieces but, if it was not the greatest work written in Europe at the time, when compared with the other two works by contemporary English composers presented at that festival – Parry's *Ode to St. Cecilia* and Frederick Bridge's *Repentance of Ninevah* – it is a masterpiece. The *Musical Times* was condescending, but basically accurate;

Mr. Elgar will do good work. He must acquire greater coherence of ideas, and conciseness of utterance – those inevitable signs of a master, only to be attained by extended and arduous effort. For such effort, no doubt, Mr. Elgar may be trusted. *Froissart* was much applauded – the Prophet had honour even in his own country.

On August 8th Novello's agreed to publish it, which meant that for the first time an Elgar première was to have properly engraved parts ready. In the middle of the preparations, on August 14th, Alice gave birth to a daughter. Following their penchant for anagrams and puzzles they named her Carice, amalgamating her mother's first two names. Elgar was, predictably, thrilled though he was distracted by the demands of *Froissart*; but he still found time for more everyday tasks: 'All is going well here & I have been promoted to nurse my offspring – a fearful joy & fatal to trousers . . . I would as soon nurse an 'automatic irrigator'. But it's a pretty little thing.'

Carice with her mother. The proud father remarked, 'I would sooner nurse an automatic irrigator'.

Living in London meant entertaining often. Visitors like the Fittons and Alice's other great friends, the Bakers, were welcome, and even her aunt Gertrude, the forbidding Dowager Lady Thompson, deigned to confer favour with one of her duty visits to 'poor relations'. However, it soon became clear that more than Alice's pearls and the odd fee for sheet music was needed to bring in the money necessary to live properly (which in those days involved employing two maids as well as running the house) and so Elgar started making weekly trips to Malvern to teach the violin again. When he had left in such hopeless than two years before, he had handed over his pupils to a German teacher, Hans Sück (who repaid the favour ten years later by conducting the first London performance of *Froissart* in St. James's Hall) and Elgar had to begin finding employment all over again. The most regular work came to be at 'The Mount', one of those respectable colleges for young ladies that Malvern seems to attract like wasps to a jam jar.

By December the added burden of a child was beginning to tell on his finances. He began to go up to Malvern more often, sometimes staying there for three days a week. Neither was the creative outlook any better. As usual the effort of a major piece had left him stale and depressed. He started a violin concerto but abandoned it. The winter was cold, the London fogs were at their gloomiest, and the strain again began to affect his health. It was becoming abundantly clear that the attempt to storm the capital had failed to

Forli, Alexandra Road, Malvern Link. When the experiment of living in London proved uneconomic it was to this place that Elgar retreated.

provide fame and fortune quick enough. During the first months of 1891 the house in Kensington was re-let and in June they retreated, disappointed and bitter, to Malvern. In fairness it had not been a total disaster by any means. With several London performances and published works to his credit Elgar was beginning to be known in the wider musical world as a composer, but not yet an established 'name'. At the time however, nothing seemed to have changed since before his marriage. He was back as a provincial tutor and a hack conductor of amateur orchestral societies.

A house in Alexandra Road, Malvern Link was taken and named 'Forli' after the Italian painter, Melozzo da Forli, medieval portrayer of angelic musicians. Hazeldine House, Alice's old home, was sold off, as was the furniture not required for the new home. However she kept many of her father's Indian bits and pieces. Rosa Burley, a young teacher who had recently taken over the post of Headmistress at 'The Mount' and was a frequent visitor and close friend for the next few years, described the interior of the modest house which . . .

suggested a taste and a culture that could not have been guessed from its somewhat suburban exterior. The dining room was on the right of the door as one entered, the drawing room, bigger because of its bay window, on the left. The little study . . . at the back, to the left of the staircase. Each contained a number of fine pieces of Indian carved furniture. In the drawing room were a few curios of which I remember a case of scented Tonkin beans and a collections of letters in Hindu script encased in the beautiful silk bag with green tassles in which they had journeyed from one prince to another.

With the proceeds from the disposal of Hazeldine and the fees Elgar collected from teaching, playing and selling the odd manuscript, they were, if still struggling, better off than they had been in London. Once settled in Malvern Elgar settled down to serious composition almost immediately. Wanting to follow the success of *Froissart* with something even bigger to assault the Festival market, he began to sketch a secular cantata (he called it a symphony for chorus and orchestra). For a text he turned to a source which continued the theme of chivalry and which had been a favourite since childhood: Longfellow's translation of a ballad by Uhland, *Der Schwarze Ritter* (The Black Knight) from 'Hyperion'.

The big choral societies at that time held the key to both financial success and national esteem, dominated, as the English musical taste was throughout the nineteenth century, by a passion for oratorio and cantata. This passion can be traced to three facets, not necessarily laudable, in the English character. As a nation the response to music tends to be emotional rather than intellectual.

The average reaction, unlike the German or French but similar to the Italian, looks for warmth rather than form, message or craftsmanship as the criterion by which to judge the worth of a work. It is interesting that Purcell turned to Corelli rather than Lully as a model, and Handel found that it was the Italian opera that found most favour in London. A logical development is that the bigger the sound, and therefore the more direct the impact to the gut rather than to the head, the more popular the music will be. Secondly, using a large chorus not only enabled the largest possible number to indulge in amateur music-making at any one time, it also increased enormously the potential market for the sale of tickets to family and friends, a form of blackmail that orchestras are not good at, but which chorus members practise with enthusiastic efficiency. Lastly, there has always been a Puritan element in English society that regards pleasure sought for no other reason as self-indulgent and therefore a sinful waste of time. Since the staple diet of the choral society was the sacred oratorios of Mendelssohn and Handel, the Victorian moralist could hide his sentimental enjoyment of music under a veil of edification. That scant attention was actually paid to the words is surely shown by the standard of the doggerel that most English composers used as texts. Elgar, though undoubtedly sincere in the sentiments he professed, was no exception. Apart from the three great sacred oratorios, the majority of the verse he set in *The Black Night, King Olaf, Caractacus, The Music Makers* and many other works, is often banal and sometimes plain mawkish. One stanza from *The Black Knight* should make the point:-

Pipe and viol call the dances
Torch-light through the high hall glances;
waves a mighty shadow in;
With manner bland
Doth ask the maiden's hand,
Doth with her the dance begin

There is no doubt that this sort of third-rate verse, though good currency at the time and reflecting the prevailing middle-class taste, has handicapped the revival of many of his works since. It has been suggested by the biographer Thomas Dunhill, amongst others, that since the orchestral writing holds most of the musical interest a purely instrumental arrangement, especially of *The Black Knight*, would make a considerable amount of Elgar's discarded music acceptable and welcome to twentieth-century audiences. Even Purcell was more fortunate with his poets.

In 1891, therefore, it was plain that while orchestral music would win recognition in London, something choral was needed for the more lucrative provinces, but he was determined not to write anything that could be dismissed as just another festival cantata. He treated the text more as a dramatic symphonic programme, writing; 'it's not a proper cantata as the orch: is too important'. He had an ally now in the young organist who had succeeded William Done at Worcester Cathedral, Hugh Blair, whose innovative energy was a welcome contrast to the old regime. He was a frequent visitor to 'Forli' and he and Elgar started orchestral services in the Cathedral on Sunday evenings. He was also the sort of friend whom Elgar most needed; a professional musician who could provide sincere critical support and tangible help for the music. 'If you will finish it,' he said when he looked through parts of *The Black Knight* on a visit in June 1892, 'I will produce it at Worcester'.

For the summer Mary Baker had organised a joint expedition to Germany but in the meantime he had finished work on the *Serenade for Strings* (which he always declared to be his own favourite work) and dispatched it to Breitkopf of Leipzig, for publication. The depression was now all gone. Buoyed up by this, and the fact that the vocal score of *The Black Knight* was safely planted at Novello's and would be performed by Blair, the Elgars left for the Continent in August. They made for the Rhine valley, visiting Cologne and Beethoven's birthplace in Bonn, and then cut across to Bayreuth by way of Mainz. Having saturated themselves with Wagner (*Meistersinger, Tristan und Isolde* and two performances of *Parsifal*) they explored the countryside; the mountains and woods of the Bavarian Highlands. 'There are large pine forests and it is so lovely to walk about in them' he wrote home to his niece, May Grafton, 'There are no hedges at all but like an open field as far as you see'. On the way home they visited the old university town of Heidelberg, and Nuremberg, where they went again to the opera, this time to see Mascagni's nearly new *Cavalleria Rusticana*.

The publication of the *Serenade for Strings*, which must rank with Grieg's *Holberg Suite* and Dvořák's *Serenade in E* as one of the finest and most popular works for string orchestra ever written, and the encouraging remarks made by Novello's about *The Black Knight* and *The Spanish Serenade* (a part song with small orchestral accompaniment) was a source of considerable encouragement to Elgar. He arrived home 'fired with songs'. Alice also was poetically inspired and together they worked on songs for the last week of August. They visited Germany for all the next three summers and gradually built up a set between them which became the *Songs from the Bavarian Highlands* – their most complete and lengthy collaboration.

Gloom came down again briefly in September when Scap, the

The Bavarian Highlands where the Elgars spent most of their summer holidays in the first ten years of their marriage.

collie he had been given by Charles Buck eight years before, died. However he was soon back at work on *The Black Knight* which was finally accepted by Novello's on 11th November and he orchestrated it through the winter. On 14th April Hugh Blair duly conducted the first performance in the Shire Hall with the Worcester Festival Choral Society, and found moderate favour with the press. It is the first of Elgar's large scale choral works and is only really remarkable for the variety of the orchestral colour, but it does show the Continental influences that he was gradually moulding into his own individual style. There is virtually nothing in the orchestra that acknowledges any debt to the prevailing academic English style of Parry or Mackenzie. The influences are far more cosmopolitan. The woodwind writing looks to Dvořák and the brass to Brahms, but he shows himself, in the orientalism of the third scene, to be very much one of his European generation, with hints of the bright sounds of Rimsky-Korsakov and even a look forward to Strauss' *Salome*. The choral writing, however, is so obviously the orchestra's poor relation that it is almost superfluous.

A few days earlier, the Herefordshire Philharmonic Society had given the première of the *Spanish Serenade*, with words also from Longfellow, in Hereford Cathedral; Elgar at his place leading the orchestra. Rosa Burley, who was in the 'comfortably large and well-dressed audience', remembered it for its haunting 'suggestion of guitars and southern warmth' as well as for the two loud-spoken ladies who sat behind her lamenting the lapse of social taste that Alice had committed by marrying a 'mere musician', and discussing the awkward situation it had made for her hierarchically-minded friends, who 'naturally felt that they could not be expected to meet a man whose father kept a wretched little house in Worcester and even tuned their pianos'. They were, it seems however, perfectly prepared to pay to hear and applaud his music. Such were the idiocies of English provincial society.

That summer's trip to Bavaria became quite a gathering (with Edward the only male in the party) for, apart from Alice, there were Rosa Burley, her pupil Alice Davey and the nineteen year old Dora Penny, soon to be stepdaughter of Mary Baker with whom Carice had been deposited for the duration of the holiday. The Elgars left England on 2nd of August and went first to the little town of Garmisch in the highlands, which they had visited briefly the previous year, and from there they hurried to Munich for the Musikfest, arriving on 17th August, where they joined Alice Davey and Rosa Burley who had already settled in. At the festival they immersed themselves once again in Wagner; all of *The Ring, Tannhäuser, Die Meistersinger, Tristan und Isolde* and even *Die Feen* at the Hoftheater, conducted by Herman Levi, were heard. The holiday brought out the best in Elgar. He was lively, boisterous and self-confident. His impish sense of humour was at its most provoking. He shocked his wife, and entertained the others, by refusing to act like a docile member of good society. On one occasion, as they sat eating sausages in a restaurant, Alice talked reverently about *Die Meistersinger* and mentioned Hans Sachs: 'what a darling old man he was', she said. 'Yes, but I expect he blew his nose with his fingers', he replied gleefully. Alice was appalled, 'Oh Edu – we won't dwell on that'. Meanwhile his German was improving (his wife's was already excellent) if not yet perfect. He told with relish of how he had taken a horse-drawn tram and, wanting to go to the last stop had asked for the 'letzte Ruhe Platz' (literally – 'the last resting place') and was rather disconcerted to find himself dropped at the cemetery! He was working though, taking notes of everything he heard and, exhorted by Alice, spending plenty of time at his desk. 'Doesn't she keep

Rosa Burley,
headmistress of The
Mount in Malvern.

him at it!' Alice Davey remarked, putting her finger straight on the point of the marriage's success.

He would, no doubt, have preferred to stay in Germany and go back into the highlands with Rosa Burley for the rest of the summer but at the end of the month he had to be in Worcester again for the Three Choirs Festival. This time there was none of his music in the programme despite Hugh Blair's enthusiasm; the main English work being Parry's *Job*, and Elgar was only engaged in his role as a member of the first violins in the festival orchestra. As soon as the week's music was out of the way for another year term had started and it was back to the grind of school teaching, for there were unwilling pupils in almost every establishment in Malvern with whom he grudgingly spent an hour a week. He was once more despondent and certain that composition was futile. As much as possible of the autumn was spent playing golf with Richard Baxter Townshend or H.D. Acland, a member of the Worcester Philharmonic (when he wasn't being a local bank manager). Elgar was determined that at least he wouldn't *look* like a penniless violin master, refusing to carry a violin case unless it was absolutely necessary. He upset the proper sentiments of various headmistresses by turning up for lessons dressed in golfing 'plus-fours', much to the delight of the girls. He was not a popular teacher with the beginners he took though, being uninterested in drilling in the basic technique and unable to bear the stumbling efforts of those who weren't accomplished players. This wasn't helped by his habit of choosing pieces that he wanted to hear rather than ones they could play. When Rosa Burley arrived at 'The Mount' she found it was 'the custom for each pupil at the end of her lesson to telegraph the state of the emotional atmosphere to her successor and there was one child who enraged him to such an extent that the others had begged that she might be placed last on the list in order to prevent her from making things impossible for them'.

Through the early part of 1894 he did little composition, concentrating on his immediate commitments or playing chamber music. Winifred Norbury, the Fitton sisters, Basil Nevinson, Hew Stewart-Powell and George Sinclair, the organist at Hereford Cathedral, were all regular visitors when there was music to play at home. In February Novellos took a part-song to Alice's words, *Happy Eyes*, and in April the visit of the Duke of York to Worcester prompted a piece for brass, strings and organ, *Sursum Corda*, which was first played in the Cathedral on the evening of the visit. Elgar was to have conducted but another bout of his recurring throat trouble made his doctor forbid it, and armed with a prescription for sea air and a change of scene, the Elgars left the West Country for a short stay in Sussex. They explored the coast around

Chichester and Littlehampton and visited the stronghold of the Catholic tradition in England, the Cathedral and castle of the Duke of Norfolk at Arundel.

By July Elgar had sufficiently recovered in mind to begin work again and, turning once more to Longfellow for a text, sketched another romantic historical cantata based on the Saga of King Olaf. Norse mythology was going through something of a fashion at the time, stimulated by a growing interest in the verse dramas of Ibsen and Bjørnson (William Archer's championing articles on Ibsen were appearing in *The Theatrical World* throughout the first half of the decade) and by the popularity of Grieg's music, in particular *Peer Gynt*.

Once creative interest was roused he launched into what was to prove his most fertile period of the decade. August and, this time, most of September were spent at Garmisch, Carice remaining at home in the capable hands of Miss Burley, and away from the cares of England the spirit of fun took over, Edward entering wholeheartedly into musical chairs, charades and football with the children of the pension. He and Alice put more combined energy into their Bavarian Songs and, home again in the autumn, Elgar forged ahead with *King Olaf*. H.A. Acworth, a retired Indian civil servant living in Malvern, was called upon to mould Longfellow's poem into a coherent text and Charles Swinnerton Heap put the idea of commissioning the first performance to the committee of the North Staffordshire Festival at Hanley. At the tail end of the year *The Black Knight* was given further performances in Hereford and Walsall and in February 1895, at Wolverhampton. Even so it did not make any money for Novello's, but it did mean that at last Elgar's music had broken through the second performance barrier and was being given at concerts independently of the composer's own initiative or the original commission. It was always welcome to be asked for a new work but the real battle was to get beyond the novelty value of the première and into the repertory.

With the new year activity was stepped up further. *Sevilliana*, which he had written for Stockley ten years before, was to be published and Worcester asked for another choral work (this time an oratorio) for the following year's festival. At a rehearsal of *The Black Knight* in Wolverhampton Elgar had the satisfaction of being introduced to the chorus as 'a genius'. Blair also wanted another work for the visit of a delegation of American organists in June. Elgar complied with an Organ Sonata, which Blair played for the visiting professionals on 8th. According to Rosa Burley he made 'a terrible mess' of it but Elgar stoutly defended him by saying that the work was so new he had not had time to learn it properly. He further repaid Blair's kindness by orchestrating his *Advent Cantata* for him.

After the usual holiday at Garmisch his composing schedule was impressively full, for not only had he to complete two commissioned large-scale choral works in a year but also put the final touches to the *Scenes from the Bavarian Highlands*, the six partsongs for chorus and orchestra that were the most tangible results of their holidays at the little village nestling underneath the Zugspitze, later also to be the retreat of Richard Strauss. Elgar conducted them for the first time at a concert in Worcester on April 21st 1896, much to Alice's delight. Later he arranged three of them (*The Dance, Lullaby* and *The Marksman*) for orchestra alone. These, more so than the original songs, were an immense success; vital, light and sounding less 'English' than anything he had written, they fitted neatly into concert programmes. The complete set, on the other hand, survived in the repertory only a short time, perhaps because although the music has easily stood the test of time, Alice's poems have not.

The work for the Three Choirs Festival of 1896 was altogether a grander affair than *Froissart* had been. It was to be his first religious oratorio and for a libretto he turned to the Rev. Edward Capel-Cure (husband of his old pupil Hilda Fitton). The orchestral rehearsal for *Lux Christi* (subtitled *The Light of Life* for die-hard Protestants) in London's Queen's Hall on September 3rd was attended by, among others, the Master of the Queen's Music, Sir Walter Parratt. The country's musical aristocracy were finally sitting up and taking notice of the emergent genius who would, within ten years, have overtaken the reputations of all of them. The oratorio, first performed on 10th, went down well with the Festival audience and five days later the Elgars entertained Dr. Heap to lunch. With him came Charles Villiers Stanford, then amongst the first rank of the nation's composers. With Elgar he looked through the score of *King Olaf*, wishing 'Good luck to yr. Norseman' in a letter just before the first night.

Dr. Heap, who was one of the most useful and best qualified of English provincial choral conductors (having studied in Leipzig on a Mendelssohn scholarship) had invited Elgar to conduct it in Hanley. The result was a near calamity, for the main soloist, the tenor Edward Lloyd, missed the last rehearsal. Elgar was exceptionally nervous on this occasion and things began to go badly wrong at the words 'And King Olaf heard the cry' and the disintegration was only halted by the leader who, overruling the rostrum, stood up and restored order with his bow. Elgar, in one of his more unreasonable moods, blamed Heap for Lloyd's lateness; a piece of ingratitude for which Heap did not forgive the composer. However the work was in fact a great success, and even more than *The Black Knight*, earned him the respect of the profession. Within a little over a year it had been performed by Manns at

Charles Villiers Stanford (1852-1924). Although at the beginning their relationship was friendly it cooled after Stanford wrote Elgar what the latter regarded as an insulting letter. (Mary Evans Lib.)

the Crystal Palace and by choral societies in Worcester, Liverpool, Bradford and Bishop Auckland as well as gaining a second hearing at Hanley.

Before Elgar conducted the work at Hanley he had relaxed at the Rev. Alfred Penny's house in Wolverhampton. He was a keen sportsman (having thoroughly enjoyed, as well as golf on the links around Malvern, taking part in a cricket match in the unlikely setting of Bavarian Garmisch) and an equally keen supporter of Wolverhampton Wanderers, so the prelude to *King Olaf* was a happy afternoon spent watching football. Midlands soccer also interrupted the smooth running of the work's London première the following April, when the Cup Final between Aston Villa and Everton (played nearby at Sydenham) not only swamped Rosa Burley and her demure young ladies from 'The Mount' in fans but also, as one critic pointed out, explained the rather reduced numbers of the choir. Appreciating that, if a choice between new music and the Cup Final was to be made, the former doesn't stand a chance, Elgar greeted the story with shouts of laughter.

Meanwhile *King Olaf* was published and specially-bound copies presented to the Kings of Norway and Sweden. 1897 was a year devoted to royalty for in that year, with much genuine rejoicing, the country threw itself vigorously into the party mood for Queen Victoria's Diamond Jubilee. Elgar, a life long Conservative and ardent supporter of the crown, was no exception and here, for the first time, we see the Public Elgar; the Elgar of *Land of Hope and Glory*, Coronation anthems and Empire Day Parades. To those who knew nothing of his serious music, the image of the erect country gentleman writing for massed bands and royal occasions became, as he grew older and gathered the rewards of state, more and more ingrained in the public mind. It was only a small part of him in reality and he hated the trivialisation that 'public ownership' inevitably entailed. In 1897, however, the enthusiasm for his patriotic cantata *The Banner of St. George* and his *Imperial March* was welcome recognition. The march was played not only at the Crystal Palace but also at a Royal Garden Party, a State Concert and (played by the Royal Artillery Band) at the Albert Hall. At home in the West Country his *Te Deum* and *Benedictus* (composed during the spring) consolidated his reputation at the Three Choirs, held under George Sinclair's directorship that year at Hereford. But chiefly it was a time for enjoying the hard-won fame, insecure

Outside Buckingham
Palace for Queen
Victoria's Jubilee in 1897.
(Mary Evans Lib.)

as it still was, and relaxing in the spirit of the Jubilee; watching the bonfires lit on the common, or kite flying, a passion ideal for the stiff breezes on the Malverns, with Troyte Griffith and Carice, seven years old that August.

The summer before, in the hectic period just before the premières of *Lux Christi* and *King Olaf*, R.J. Buckley, who was to be Elgar's first biographer, went to visit him at 'Forli'. The hedge of the lawn before the house was in flower.

Close at hand was a larger lawn . . . whereon was a sunny tent, the opening of which commanded a glorious valley, extending to the purple horizon . . . We took our seats in this ideal retreat where were easy chairs, a table and a couch which reminded me of Rossini dashing off operas in bed . . . Overflowing with enthusiasm, he spoke rapidly and continuously of the state of musical art in England, deploring the fate of works commissioned for festivals, which, after painstaking and elaborate production, were heard no more. His bearing was that of one in deadly earnest . . . too intent on his aim to waste time on anything not directly leading to his goal . . . The tent was littered with sheets of music paper bearing myriad pencil marks undecipherable to the stranger. Of a fugue in 'The Light of Life' he said: 'I thought a fugue would be expected of me. The British public would hardly tolerate oratorio without fugue. So I tried to give them one' . . . Questioned as to his actual feeling for the perpetuation of the fugal style, he rose and walked rapidly about, as is his custom when interested. 'It has been done,' he said. 'Bach has done it. No man has a greater reverence for Bach than I. But my veneration for Bach is no reason why I should imitate Bach. I certainly can't beat Bach in the Bach manner . . . My idea is that there is music in the air, music all around us, the world is full of it and – (here he raised his hands and made a rapid gesture of capture) – and – you – simply – simply take as much of it as you require.'

During the middle months of 1897 August Johannes Jaeger became prominent in Elgar's life for the first time. He was a meticulous and tenacious editor and his boundless sympathy for both Elgar and his music, as well as his sound professional criticism, probably had a greater influence on Elgar's music during the period of his finest work than that of any other man. Jaeger, three years younger than Elgar, was born in Düsseldorf, but had come to England in 1878 and joined Novellos in 1890. The fact that he was German immediately earned him the composer's respect, but this was heightened, mutually, by the realisation that they were both outside the mainstream of English music. 'I am conceited enough to think', Jaeger wrote after attending the first performance of the *Te Deum*, 'that I can appreciate a good thing and see genius in musicians that are *not* yet dead, or even not yet well known, or Cathedral organists, or Directors of music in colleges for boys.' That confidence was the basis of the most valuable friendship either ever found.

In December Elgar received a commission for the following autumn's Leeds Festival; then, with Birmingham, the most prestigious of the country's platforms for new music. It was by far the most important sign of national recognition he had yet had and he wanted to write a symphony, an ambition that was to become almost obsessive over the next decade. The Leeds committee, though, knew him as a composer of choral extravaganzas and that was what they wanted. For a subject Elgar turned once more to his mother, the inspiration of so much of his early music, and to the heritage of Worcestershire's hills. 'On going out we stood at the door looking along the back of the hills', Anne Elgar wrote to Edward's sister, Polly, 'the Beacon was in full view – I said Oh! Ed. Look at the lovely old hill. Can't we write some tale about it. I quite long to have something worked up about it . . . you can "do it yourself Mother" He held my hand with a firm grip "do" he said – no I can't my day is gone by if ever I could and so we parted – and in less than a month he told me *Caractacus* was all cut and dried – and he had begun to work at it – that's the story – So I feel a sort of Godmother to it.'

For once there was no possibility of setting Longfellow but he persisted in finding doggerel, this time from the treasurer of the Golf Club, Henry Acworth, who had pruned *King Olaf*. The result was less disastrous than it might have been, but the words were still inadequate and sentimental as Jaeger was not slow to point

The view across the valleys of the Rivers Teme and Severn from Birchwood, looking North East towards Birmingham. (photo: Jane Whitton).

out. The finale is especially jingoistic: the Romans, having captured the valiant Caractacus, sing of the glorious future when the British empire will replace their own. Elgar faced Jaeger's criticism unrepentently:

I *did* suggest that we should dabble in patriotism in the Finale, when lo! the 'worder' (that's good!) instead of merely paddling his feet goes and gets naked and wallows in it: now I don't think he meant by 'menial &c' Germany &c. more probably hill tribes and suchlike . . . Now 'pluck ye by the ear' if you feel aggrieved, I will bring my sword up & give as pretty a fight as you can wish . . . but I warn I am probably a better swordsman than you.

Caractacus occupied him throughout the spring of 1898 and he did most of the writing at Birchwood Lodge, the keeper's cottage they had rented as a retreat about three miles from Malvern. The small white house, perched on a stirrup of the Malverns just across the valley of the River Teme into Herefordshire from his birthplace at Broadheath, was an idyllic setting and is still aloof from the bustle of Worcester and the Severn. Elgar was never so happy as when let loose in the countryside and for Carice as well Birchwood held the happiest associations:-

The cottage had several rooms and the well was immediately outside the front fence, and we drew the water – beautiful clear water – up in a large bucket. On one side of the cottage we walked straight into a lovely wood. In a tree close to the house Father had an elaborate system of traps for

Birchwood. Elgar stands in the garden looking towards the camera.

37

wasps and even hornets, which he looked after every day, putting fresh syrup and so on . . . Another great enjoyment here was the making of paths through the woods, and when I was at home, I was allowed to help, following and picking up the odd branches as he cut them off.

That August Elgar wrote to Jaeger,

I say I wish you were here! I've been cutting a long path thro' the dense jungle like primitive man only with more clothes. But you will see our woodlands someday. I made old Caractacus stop as if broken down on page 168 & choke & say 'woodlands' again because I am so madly devoted to my woods. I've got the place for years now & another summer – ja!

Caractacus was first performed in Leeds on 5th October 1898 and dedicated to Queen Victoria. It was not the most perfect rendering but, even so, Elgar found that he was now a celebrity. The Lord Mayor invited him to lunch and among the musical famous who attended the performance were Fauré, Stanford, Parry, Cowen and Sir Arthur Sullivan, then sick and in his last season as festival conductor (for which he had to sit) but he insisted on attending Elgar's rehearsals to help and make notes. 'You may say of him' wrote the critic of the *Musical Standard* much to Elgar's delight, 'with truth that he writes *music*.'

Sir Arthur Sullivan (1842-1900). Although ill in 1898 he was still determined to attend the rehearsals for Caractacus.

As he entered his forties Elgar was equal in reputation to the most admired musicians in the country. A programme note from a Worcester Festival concert of 1896 sums it up:- 'Elgar ranks in the estimation of all competent judges amongst the most able and promising of the younger generation of composers'. Henry Wood added, 'Most of us thought that, in time, he would give us great works, but few guessed *how* great they would prove to be.'

However his reputation was advancing, though, his finances were in as desperate a state as ever. 1897 had been his best year to date for performances yet at the end of it he wrote to Jaeger,

I have some ideas: but am talking about taking a new house – *very noisy* close to the station where I *can't write* at all but will be more convenient for pupils to come in – I have no intention of bothering myself with music. Look here! in two years I have written Lux Xti, King Olaf, Impl. March, St. George, Organ Sonata (big), Te Deum. Recd £86-15., Debtor £100 after paying my own expenses at two festivals I feel a d–d fool! (English expression) for thinking of music at all. No amount of 'kind encouragement' can blot out these simple figures. Ever yours Ed. Elgar.

3 From Enigma to Knighthood

On 24th October 1898, Elgar wrote from Malvern to Jaeger in the following terms:

> . . . Our woods look lovely but decidedly damp and rheumaticky – unromantic just now.
>
> Since I've been back I have sketched a set of Variations (orkestra) on an original theme: the Variations have amused me because I've labelled 'em with the nicknames of my particular friends – *you* are Nimrod. That is to say I've written the variations each one to represent the mood of the 'party' – I've liked to imagine the 'party' writing the var: him (or her) self and have written what I think they wd. have written – if they were asses enough to compose – it's a quaint idea and the result is amusing to those behind the scenes and won't affect the hearer who 'nose nuffin'. What think you? Much love and sunshine to you.
> Ed. Elgar.

So began the composition of Elgar's Op. 36, The *Enigma* Variations, perhaps still the best known of his music, especially abroad, and certainly the work, with its typical 'crossword' puzzle, that has occupied the largest portion of interesting speculation. There are fourteen variations in all, twelve headed by the initials of a close friend. The first depicts C.A.E., his wife, Alice, the last is of himself.

Elgar loved words and their possible contortions all his life and the work's 'Enigma' subtitle is just, perhaps, the most insoluble of all his puzzles. The problems arose from the composer's programme note to the first performance.

> The enigma I will not explain – it's 'dark saying' must be left unguessed, and I warn you that the apparent connection between the variations and the theme is often of the slightest texture: further, through and over the whole set another and larger theme 'goes', but is not played.

What that 'larger' theme is Elgar obstinately never revealed. In fact the longer it continued unsolved, the less he seemed inclined to spoil the mystery. Some of the suggestions for the counterpointed melody are Chopin's G minor Nocturne, Stanford's *Requiem*, and a Bach motet. Among the more outlandish are *Home, Sweet Home, Auld Lang Syne* (Elgar himself debunked that one) and *Ta-ra-ra-boom-de-ay*. We shall, of course, never know for certain now and it seems almost irrelevant to the music. Indeed if the enigma was solved something of the work's charm might be lost. The puzzle really is more interesting in relation to Elgar's character than to the substance of his work. It is doubtful even whether he thought of the enigmatic possibilities until the work was finished, for the subtitle does not appear until May 1899, the month before the first performance, at least seven months after its gestation.

Elgar worked on the Variations intermittently all through the Autumn at Birchwood. He was already thinking about possible Festival commissions for the following year. On 11th November he wrote again to Jaeger;

The Variations go on slowly but I shall finish them some day. I have agreed to do the principal novelty for Birmingham . . . Then, *un*officially, poor old Worcester wants a symphony. You see that none of this will pay me a cent.

The 'novelty' for Birmingham was eventually to become *The Dream of Gerontius*, a project Elgar had been working on in his mind for some years. But meanwhile he concentrated on the Variations and conducting work for the Worcestershire Philharmonic Society. He was also having a dispute with Novello's, his publishers, who evidently were reluctant to guarantee the returns on his serious work.

The only suggestion made is that the Henry VIII dances, [by Edward German], are the thing – now I can't write that sort of thing and my own heartfelt ideas are not wanted: why K. Olaf should be worthless when it's done often is a mystery to me when things by, say, Mackenzie, which are never touched, shd. be good properties. You see I want so little: £300 a year I must make, and that's all. Last year I subsisted on £200. It seems strange that a man who might do good work shd. be absolutely stopped. That's what it means.

By February 1899 the orchestration of *Enigma* was well advanced as were plans to move from 'Forli' to a house in Wells Road, Malvern. On 21st Elgar took what was to prove a decisive step in his career. In the hope of interesting Hans Richter, the most influential foreigner and, as conductor of The Hallé Orchestra, the most revered patriarch involved in English

The manuscript of the
Enigma Variations,
Variation IX. Nimrod,
opening bars.

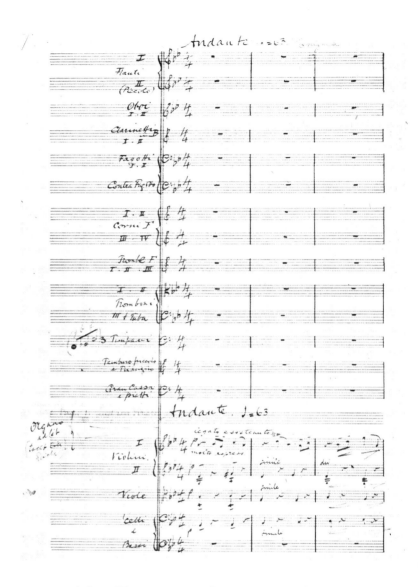

concert-giving, Elgar sent the finished score of his *Variations* to
Nathaniel Vert, Richter's manager. The idea was that the new
piece should be performed at one of Richter's concerts in London.
Elgar was excited but also uncertain about the great man's likely
reaction, and urged Jaeger not to set too much store by his success:

. . . for mercy's sake don't tell *anyone* I pray you about Richter becos' he
may refuse. Vert is keen about it and it would be just too lovely for
anything if R. did an English piece by a man who hasn't appeared yet . . .

March saw the move to the new home. The Elgars, as ever
enjoying the intricacies of words, concocted an anagram of their
initials and came up with the name 'Craeg Lea'. Here, and at their
country retreat at Birchwood Lodge, they lived until 1904.

Lady Mary Lygon, organiser of the music festivals at Madresfield Court.

All through the early months of 1899 Elgar was frantically busy. Not only was he coping with the business of moving house, he also had to correct the proofs of *Three Characteristic Pieces*, the *Variations*, and *Caractacus*, which he was due to conduct at the Albert Hall on 20th April. The three pieces he dedicated to Lady Mary Lygon, sister of Lord Beauchamp, who was about to go to New Zealand where her brother was the new Governor. Lady Mary ran the local music festival that took place at Madresfield Court, her family's Tudor stately-home just outside Malvern. The festival was mostly an amateur affair and naturally a local musician like Elgar was very much involved. The Lygon family soon became valued friends, the first aristocrats to recognise Elgar for his musical, rather than his wife's social, credentials. 'She is a most angelic person', said Elgar, 'and I should like to please her – there are few who deserve pleasing . . .'

At that time he also put the finishing touches to his orchestrated song cycle, 'Sea Pictures' on which he had worked since 1897. For contralto voice, these five songs may now seem rather dated in their sentimental and at times jingoistic words, but the orchestration, as with everything he wrote that year, remains fresh and masterly, while No. 4, *Where Corals Lie*, contains one of his most haunting melodies.

Negotiations with Vert for a Richter première of the *Variations* went well and by April Elgar could report to Jaeger that he had 'rote . . . asking to be in a Joon programme if humanly possible': and so it proved. In the meantime Henry Wood conducted the first London performance of the *Meditation* from *Lux Christi* at the Queen's Hall. It was the first concert of that year's London Musical Festival, the opening half of which consisted of the British première of a new work by Dukas – *The Sorcerer's Apprentice* – conducted by Charles Lamoureux, the veteran Parisian conductor on his last visit to England. There were tribulations though. His daughter was sent home from school suffering from whooping cough, (a worry for any parent at the turn of the century) and he was unhappy with the *Caractacus* concert. Moreover the haggling over royalties with Novello's continued. In this case it was his cantata *The Black Knight* which was deemed uncommercial. Elgar's reply was to the point:

I see how it is. I think it is too artistic for the ordinary conductor of Choral Societies – I find that they are an inordinately ignorant lot of cheesemongering idiots.

At last on 19th June the *Enigma Variations* were given their first performance under Hans Richter in St. James's Hall. It was a huge success and even Elgar, with his obsessive sense of neglect, could

Hew David
Stewart-Powell,
Variation II.

Richard Baxter
Townshend,
Variation III.

William Meath Baker,
Variation IV.

not help but be pleased with the reaction. The musical press was as ecstatic and *The Musical Times* positively effusive;

Effortless originality – the only true originality – combined with thorough savoir faire and, most important of all, beauty of theme, warmth and feeling are his credentials, and they should open to him the hearts of all who have faith in the future of our English art and appreciate beautiful music wherever it is met.

The warmth of this criticism is rather less than surprising since the writer was none other than Jaeger, himself one of the *Variations'* dedicatees.

However, his optimism proved to be justified. Once championed by Richter, Elgar graduated in the public's mind from being just another, albeit fairly successful, composer of salon pieces and provincial festival commissions to become a banner of hope to those looking for a new voice in the rather turgid mass of English music. As Buckley wrote three years later:

The Enigma Variations, toured by Richter's band, set the seal on Elgar's reputation. Richter did for Elgar what he had done for Wagner thirty years before. England was won for Wagner by Richter and the *Tannhäuser* Overture. England was won for Elgar by Richter and *The Enigma Variations*.

Although the *Variations* stand independently of their programmes, the friends whose initials were placed at the head of each have become an inherent part of the Elgar myth. After the opening statement of the theme and the first variation depicting Alice comes 'H.D.S-P.' – Hew David Stewart-Powell – one of the group that used to gather in the Elgar household to play chamber-music: Stewart-Powell was the pianist whose 'diatonic run over the keys', Elgar wrote later in notes for a set of piano rolls made by the Aeolian Company, 'before beginning to play is here humorously travestied in the semiquaver passages; these should suggest a Toccata, but chromatic beyond H.D.S-P.'s liking.'

Richard Baxter Townshend (R.B.T., Variation III) was an eccentric who rode a tricycle and with whom Elgar played golf, but he was also married to one of the sisters of William Meath Baker (Variation IV), who often entertained the Elgars at his country mansion, Hasfield Court. Baker was one of the most loyal of Alice's gentry friends who, with his sisters, had stood by her after her marriage. Like many of the variations, this one refers to a specific incident. 'In the days of horses and carriages it was more difficult than in these days of petrol to arrange the carriages for the day to suit a large number of guests. This Variation was written after the host had, with slip of paper in hand, forcibly read out the arrangements for the day and hurriedly left the music room with an inadvertent bang of the door. In bars 15-24 are some suggestions of the teasing attitude of the guests.'

The fifth variation portrays Richard Arnold, son of the poet Matthew Arnold, a music-lover and self-taught pianist who, when he played, evaded the difficulties but suggested 'in a mysterious way the real feeling. His serious conversation was continually broken by whimsical and witty remarks.' Isobel Fitton comes sixth; tall and statuesque, one of the family through which Elgar was introduced to Alice.

VII depicts the 'maladroit essays to play the pianoforte' of Arthur Troyte Griffith, an architect and artist who was Elgar's closest non-musical friend for over thirty years. He was always ready to partner the composer in whatever 'japes' were on hand, kite-flying and bicycling being chief among them. Above all they shared their love of the Worcestershire countryside and, in later

Richard Arnold,
Variation V.

Isobel Fitton (Ysobel),
Variation VI.

Arthur Troyte Griffith
(Troyte), Variation VII.

Winifred Norbury,
Variation VIII.

August Johannes Jaeger
(Nimrod), Variation IX.

years, when Elgar offered him the chance of joining a London club, it was rejected. Troyte preferred to remain and sketch the Malverns. The energy of this exuberant variation has all the 'banter' of Troyte's boisterous good humour.

In the eighth variation, W.N., the graciousness of the 18th Century country mansion of the Norbury family is shown, though it is Winifred, the most musical and an active force in the Worcestershire Philharmonic Society, who actually receives credit at the top of the score.

Nimrod, Variation IX, is the most famous of all the movements, a noble tribute to Jaeger, Elgar's confidant and most influential helper. The occasion remembered was 'a long summer evening talk, when my friend discoursed eloquently on the slow movements of Beethoven'. In a letter on 13th March 1899 Elgar wrote 'Mrs J. will recognise your portrait quicker than you will: I have omitted your outside manner & have only seen the good, lovable

Dora Penny (Dorabella), Variation X.

Dr. George Sinclair with Dan, his bulldog, Variation XI.

honest SOUL in the middle of you! and the music's not good enough: . . .'

If Nimrod is the most famous then 'Dorabella' is the most charming. The nickname, from Mozart's *Cosi fan Tutte*, is for Dora Penny, petite and beautiful daughter of the Rector of Wolverhampton. Dorabella had been fascinated by Elgar ever since the early 1890s when, as a girl of nineteen Edward and Alice had taken her on holiday with them. She made herself useful when she went to stay, helping sort the manuscript or keeping Alice company in the long hours when the study door was locked and Elgar was composing. She was the first of the many female friends to whom he turned when he needed intelligent and attractive company outside the confines of his stable and happy, but not always inspiring, marriage.

XI actually pictures a dog called Dan, though it carries the initials of his august master, the organist of Hereford Cathedral, G.R. Sinclair. Dan's 'falling down the steep bank into the River Wye: his paddling upstream to find a landing place . . . and his rejoicing on landing prompted G.R.S. to challenge Elgar ' "Set that to music". I did; here it is'. 'B.G.N.' which follows, is Basil Nevinson, another of the group that met to play chamber music, whose house the Elgars often used whenever they had to visit London.

' * * *' is the title of Variation XIII, the subtitle being Romanza, and here we find another intriguing Elgarian puzzle. He wrote, 'the asterisks take the place of the name of a lady who was, at the time of the composition, on a sea voyage. The drums suggest the distant throb of the engines of a liner over which the clarinet quotes a phrase from Mendelssohn's "Calm Sea and Prosperous Voyage" '. The most often assumed dedicatee is Lady Mary Lygon, also the dedicatee of the 'Three Characteristic Pieces', who left for New South Wales with her brother who had been appointed Governor in May 1899. But the mood of the piece does not totally vindicate her claim. Firstly, she left many months after the work's composition. Secondly the deep romantic nature and the sudden transformations into tragedy and sadness, moments similar to those in the Second Symphony and Violin Concerto, as well as the juxtaposition next to Elgar's own variation which follows, surely points to a far more intense longing than that prompted by the temporary parting of affectionate friends? The regretful quote from the Mendelssohn could as easily be a reference to a past separation by the sea as to a future one and it was suggested by Ernest Newman that it referred to his romance with the girl from Leipzig (where Mendelssohn was conductor and one of Elgar's early idols – Elgar had sketched a 'Scotch Overture' in 1885 soon after conducting the slow movement of the 'Scottish

Basil Nevinson, Variation XII.

Symphony' in Worcester). He had certainly been deeply attached to her, naming her as his Braut (bride) in a letter to Charles Buck. It is also possible that it was for the same sentimental reason that he sent his 'Serenade' to the Leipzig publishers Breitkopf and Hartel rather than to an English firm. At an early stage in the composition he headed the 'Enigma' sketch 'L' before substituting the asterisks. This can be only conjecture now, however, and the wistful glance could have been to any of his past romances. Elgar was never averse to hiding behind shields when it seemed that questions about his emotions were probing rather deeper than he liked and so it is quite possible that he was happy to accept the excuse with which Lady Mary's voyage and respectable acquaintance provided him.

Finally, in the defiant XIVth Variation E.D.U. is Elgar himself, the initials standing for his wife's name for him, pronounced like the first part of the German 'Eduard'. This is not the Elgar either of pompous celebration or of searching intimacy, but rather the Elgar of vigour and determination to succeed.

The *Variations* were soon being performed all over the country. In July Granville Bantock conducted the work at New Brighton and later in the summer Elgar himself took the rostrum at the

Elgar and Granville Bantock: in his day an enterprising composer of the English late romantic school. He also conducted the summer concerts at New Brighton, just outside Liverpool. (Radio

Three Choirs Festival. *King Olaf*, as well, was performed at the Sheffield Festival.

The main creative work, however, now that his reputation was secure, was the commission for the Birmingham Festival of 1900. Another oratorio was required and for this Elgar was able to combine two major ideas that had been working in his mind for several years, although one of them, something based on the life of General Gordon of Khartoum, was never fully used.

One of the presents at his wedding had been a copy of Cardinal Newman's devotional poem *The Dream of Gerontius*. Father Knight's gift had one special feature which was the annotation throughout of General Gordon's favourite passages. The mysticism of Newman's verse had fascinated him, and it may have been his wife's military background or the Gordon annotations that sparked off his interest in completing the long-planned *Gerontius* project just at the time when he was being pressed by Jaeger to write a 'Gordon Symphony'. This is, however, speculation. What is certain is that on 1st January 1900 the chairman of the Birmingham Festival, G.H. Johnstone, visited Elgar at Malvern to confirm the details and terms for the performance of the new work. It was an auspicious beginning to the twentieth century.

The same month Elgar went to Manchester to conduct the Hallé in *Sea Pictures*. Once again the reviews were good: the Manchester Guardian commented:

'At the end (Miss Clara Butt) shared with the composer, who had conducted the brilliantly orchestrated accompaniments, the enthusiastic greeting of the audience. There was no mistaking the genuine enjoyment that the songs had afforded.'

Sir Charles Stanford had also conducted a piece in the same concert and Elgar had supper with him, a moment of cordiality in what was a rather bumpy relationship with a fellow composer; Elgar once remarking that 'the stuff I hate . . . is stuff like Stanford's which is neither fish, flesh, fowl, nor good red-herring.'

Throughout the rest of the winter he worked solidly on *Gerontius*, sending the first part to Jaeger on the 20th March. Jaeger was thrilled with the new work.

Since Parsifal nothing of this mystic religious kind of music has appeared to my knowledge that displays the same power and beauty as yours. Like Wagner you seem to grow with your greater, more difficult subject.

For Elgar the completion of *Gerontius* was one of the greatest strains he ever felt during composition. The poem touched all his

Elgar, having just put the final touches to The Dream of Gerontius, photographed in his study at Birchwood by William Eller.

feelings of faith and also, perhaps more importantly, reached the meditative and deeply sad aspect of his character which he had never allowed himself to express in his music before. There is more of him in this work even than in the *Enigma Variations* or any of his earlier music. He completed the short score on June 6th and the full score on August 3rd. Against the last double bar-line he wrote a quotation from Ruskin,

this is the best of me; for the rest, I ate, and drank, and slept, loved and hated, like another; my life was as the vapour, and is not; but *this* I saw and knew: this, if anything of mine, is worth your memory.

The same day his friend William Eller cycled over to see him at Birchwood. Luckily he took his camera with him and we possess what must be a very rare example of a photograph of a composer who has just finished a major work.

However, time was becoming worryingly short. The first performance in Birmingham had been fixed for 3rd October and the chorus still had to rehearse parts which, even now, with their fierce moments of attack and the often meandering harmonies, take some time to master. Above all it was difficult for an amateur choir to stay in tune. The state of readiness was not helped when, halfway through the rehearsals, Swinnerton Heap, who was the able chorus master, died and old Stockley came out of retirement. While he had been a capable conductor of Elgar's early trifles, he was now too old to be effective and did not understand or approve of his protégé's new style. The final rehearsal seems to have been chaotic, despite the efforts of Richter, who was conducting, and of Elgar himself to force it into some sort of cohesive shape. The performance was not a complete disaster, but neither was it a success and the critics, although kind enough, could not be more than tepid. The Manchester Guardian, though, in the person of the young and gifted critic, Arthur Johnstone, called the work 'Dantesque' and ended the review by admitting that, 'I am more than usually troubled by the sense of utter inadequacy in these notes, and can only hope that I may have some opportunity of doing better justice to a deeply impressive work.'

Elgar, not surprisingly, was miserable. He had counted on *Gerontius* to prove to the public that he was a serious composer and he felt a great sense of failure. A week later, he wrote to Jaeger:

As far as I am concerned music in England is dead . . . I have worked for forty years and at the last, Providence denies me a decent hearing of my work: . . . anything obscene or trivial is blessed in this world and has a reward – I ask for no reward – only to live and hear my work . . . Still it is curious to be treated by the old fashioned people as a criminal because my thoughts and ways are beyond them.

48

He was not alone in finding the attitude of the English musical establishment at the time depressing. R.J. Buckley, writing in 1904 said,

The average concert-goer was not prepared either for the strangeness of the mood or the complexity of the music . . . which demanded unwonted mental exertion. In Britain the popular notion of music is something pleasant and ear-tickling . . . English audiences are seldom inclined to be studious and therefore are rarely prepared to take serious composition with deep seriousness. Their conception of the loftiest music is, in the main, sentimental . . . with hardly a trace of the intellectual. It is this false conception which has given the name of *The Moonlight* to one of the most tragic sonatas of Beethoven. No wonder *Gerontius* fell flat.

The final months of 1900 were a thoroughly depressing time for Elgar. Alice had had to undergo a minor throat operation at the time of the *Gerontius* première and, more durably worrying, their financial position was worse than ever. He was determined that he would not go back to teaching, which he loathed, whatever the crisis but neither his conducting nor his fees and royalties, when he could get any, were producing enough. There were, however, two bright spots in the general gloom. One was the interest shown in *Gerontius* by the German conductor, Julius Buths, who translated the libretto and performed it in Düsseldorf in December of the following year. The other was the conferment in November of the degree of Mus.D. by Cambridge University. This honour, the first of many academic accolades, came at the instigation of Stanford, and was a measure of just how seriously the musical world had taken Elgar since the triumph of *Enigma*. Only a few years before, in 1893, Cambridge had awarded doctorates to Tchaikovsky, Grieg, Saint-Saëns and Max Bruch, all of whom attended in person to receive it. Elgar was now considered fit for such company, but he nearly turned down the honour. Rosa Burley says that she was called over one day by Alice Elgar to talk sense into him. She found him sitting at his table with his head in his hands writing a letter of refusal. 'I can't afford to buy the robes', he said. 'You can hire them,' she answered, 'you are not the first impecunious Doctor of Music'. Finally, November 22nd, St. Cecilia's day, was chosen for the ceremony.

The only method of relief was to lose himself in his music once more but, this time, something as far removed as possible from the mood of Gerontius, without being as trivial as the 'popular songs' that others urged on him. The result was an overture which had been suggested to him by a visit to the old Guildhall in the City of London. 'Looking at the memorials of the city's great past & knowing well the history of its unending charity, I seemed to hear

Cardinal John Henry Newman (1801-1890): from whose poem Elgar took the libretto for Gerontius.

far away in the dim roof a theme, an echo of some noble melody . . .' and to Jaeger he wrote on 4th November, 'Don't say anything about the prospective overture yet – I call it "Cockayne" and it's cheerful and Londony – "stout and steaky" '.

With the new year and the completion of *Cockaigne* on 24th March the dismal mood began to disperse, although the quotation from Langland's *Piers Plowman*, one of his favourite poems, which he appended to the manuscript of the overture's score, was highly appropriate to his situation: 'meteless and moneyless on Malvern Hills'.

Throughout the first half of 1901 Elgar's music was being performed more than ever before in concert halls not only in England, but on the Continent as well. Most gratifying of all was the fact that now it was the orchestral, rather than the choral, parts of his output that were in demand. On 7th February Buths gave the first performance in Germany of the *Variations*, in Düsseldorf, much to Jaeger's delight, since it was his native town. The reaction of the audience was enthusiastic, surprising when one considers the low opinion Continental audiences held of English music and the strained political relations of the two countries at the time. On the 16th February Elgar went to Bradford to conduct *Froissart*, four of the *Sea Pictures* and two extracts from *Gerontius*, and then came straight down to London to hear Henry Wood give the Prelude and Finale of the same work at Queen's Hall. In May the *Variations* were also given in the Queen's Hall and the following month he recognised his new academic status by directing the *Sea Pictures* at Cambridge at the suggestion of Stanford.

It was the performing side of the music that occupied Elgar for most of the early part of the year and nothing of great importance was begun. He wrote some incidental music to a play, *Grania and Diarmid*, by W.B. Yeats and George Moore, which was to be produced at the Gaiety Theatre, Dublin, in the Autumn. He had also started pulling together material for the first instalment of the *Pomp and Circumstance* marches. For most of the time, though, he worked on purely money-making orchestration of Herbert Brewer's Cantata *Emmaus* for the Three Choirs Festival that year. He did not really relish the prospect of working on other people's music, unless it was editing Bach or arranging Handel, but this work appealed to him more than most. 'Some of *Emmaus* is really beautiful and lends itself to scoring in a ready and exceptional way. I have not made what I call an elaborate score but I hope it is artistic'. Brewer, who had been ill and terrified that he would lose the commission, was desperately grateful.

With the work for Brewer out of the way the Elgars retreated to Birchwood for the summer. While they were there August Jaeger and Julius Buths, who had arranged to conduct *Gerontius* in

The title page of the original edition of the Cockaigne Overture. (Boosey & Hawkes.)

Düsseldorf that December, came to stay at 'Craeg Lea'. Elgar, meanwhile, once again settled in to the quietness of the woods that then surrounded the cottage, and worked on the marches. The famous theme for *Pomp and Circumstance: No. 1* had, it seems, come to him during the writing of *Cockaigne* earlier in the year: at the time he had thought that it might be a possible theme for the long-projected symphony. Nothing more came of it, however, but in May he had shown the new march to Dora Penny with the words 'I've got a tune that will knock'em – knock'em flat!'. He always regretted slightly using the great melody that the following year was to become 'Land of Hope and Glory' in such an unimportant work, yet of all his tunes it is the most famous. Across the world, people who have never even heard of Elgar can hum that theme whatever unfortunate images of jingoism and Empire it may now conjure up. In one way, perhaps, it would have been better used in a less conspicuous place, for through its immense popularity it earned an indelible label of complacent nationalistic pomposity for Elgar. This label is far from accurate but, I suspect, it will never be completely removed from the minds of those who know no more of his music than the *Pomp and Circumstance* marches and *Nimrod.*.

As a result of a temporary rift with Novello's, the first march was dispatched to Boosey and Hawkes for publication at the end of July and the second followed a month later. That August one of the summer visitors to Malvern was the young composer Arnold Bax, then only eighteen. George Alder, a local horn player and a friend of Bax's from his days at the Royal Academy of Music, suggested one afternoon that they walk over to Birchwood for tea. Bax's impression is one of the most lucid that we have of Elgar at this time:

Hatless, dressed in rough tweeds and riding boots, his appearance was rather that of a retired army officer turned gentleman farmer than an eminent and almost morbidly highly strung artist. One almost expected him to sling a gun from his back and drop a brace of pheasants to the ground. Refusing tea and sinking to a chair he lay back, his thin legs sprawling straight out before him, whilst he filled and lit a huge briar, his rather closely set eyes meanwhile blinking absently at us. He was not a big man, but such was the dominance of his personality that I always had the impression that he was twice as large as life. That afternoon he was very pleasant and even communicative in his rumbling voice, yet there was ever a faint sense of detachment, a hint – very slight – of hauteur and reserve. He was still sore over the *Gerontius* fiasco at Birmingham in the previous autumn, and enlarged interestingly upon the subject. 'The fact is', he said, 'neither the choir nor Richter knew the score.' 'But I thought the critics said . . .' I started to interpose. 'Critics!', snapped the composer with ferocity, 'My dear boy, what do the critics know about

Arnold Bax (1883-1953).

anything?' . . . On being told that I intended to devote myself to composition Elgar had made no comment beyond a grimly muttered, 'God help him!' . . . In the following year I was invited for the first time to send in a work for performance at a Queen's Hall Promenade Concert, and when I went to Sir Henry Wood for a preliminary run through he told me (to my intense pride) that it was none other than Elgar who had recommended him to take up my work.

On the 15th August Elgar went for a short holiday to Llangranog on the Cardiganshire (now Dyfed) coast of Wales. Rosa Burley had taken a small cottage overlooking the sea towards the island of Ynys Lochtyn. There was no room in the small cottage for Elgar as well as the Burley nephews and nieces, so he stayed with neighbours. Although the countryside of Worcestershire seems to have been essential for the development and composition of all his major music, Elgar was always at his most sociable when away from the constraints of provincial life which, with the problem of money and his ever-growing conviction that nobody wanted or understood his music, used to produce bouts of bleak depression which lasted many days. However, as Rosa Burley wrote later,

The sudden change of scene and company completely banished the depression and . . . he showed the sunniest side of his character and was delighted with everything, the scenery . . . and above all with the sea. He had been abroad of course many times but the seaside seemed to fascinate him. He had no bathing suit so we made him one out of an old pair of pyjamas; the children, with whom he made great friends, laughed and danced round him when he ventured into the water and he was not offended when one of them told him with shattering candour that he looked like a monkey.

There was a boyish streak in Elgar's character that never really disappeared with age. That summer he took Arnold Bax kite-flying – rather unsuccessfully, as there was no wind. When the Three Choirs Festival, that year at Gloucester, came round in September he struck up a long running charade with the sons of William Baker, his host at Hasfield Court, in which he played the part of Nanty Ewart, a swashbuckling figure from Sir Walter Scott's novel *Redgauntlet*.

These were not the most fruitful months of his composing life, although he did put the final touches to the *Grania and Diarmid* score. But they do seem to have been amongst the happiest days that Elgar spent. If there was a summer that lives up to the pre-conceptions of a relaxed country life in Edwardian England, it was probably that of 1901 spent in Wales and Gloucester and, above all, at Birchwood.

Friday, 11th October saw Elgar in Leeds to conduct the *Enigma Variations*, and a week later he went up to Liverpool to hear Rodewald conduct the first performance of the *Pomp and Circumstance* marches on Saturday 19th at St. George's Hall. They went well but not as well as at the London première the following Wednesday, at the Proms, under Henry Wood. Jaeger wrote to Elgar:

Your splendid marches were the greatest success I have ever witnessed over a novelty at any concert. The hall was only half full alas (though the Promenade was pretty crowded). What a pity you were not there.

Wood's account of it sets the scene better.

I shall never forget the scene at the close of the first of them. The people simply rose and yelled. I had to play it again – with the same result; in fact, they refused to let me go on with the programme. After considerable delay, while the audience roared its applause, I went off and fetched Harry Dearth who was to sing *Hiawatha's Vision*; but they would not listen. Merely to restore order, I played the march a third time. And that, I may say, was the one and only time in the history of the promenade concerts that an orchestral item was accorded a double encore.

Elgar, with the first Prom performance of the marches, had arrived as a popular, and more importantly for his future reputation, as a national composer. This was confirmed when Elgar was invited to contribute a Coronation Ode to the celebrations marking the Coronation of Edward VII, which was due to take place in June 1902. Hearing that the King had been impressed with the trio theme in *Pomp and Circumstance: No. 1* he decided to try and set words to it. For this he contacted A.C. Benson and by December 10th he had completed the first draft of *Land of Hope and Glory*.

Jaeger was less than enthusiastic about the idea.

You will have to find another tune for the ode . . . I have been trying much to fit words to it. That drop to E and the bigger drop afterwards are quite impossible in singing any words to them, they sound downright vulgar. Just try it. The effect is fatal . . . Consider carefully and give no choir a chance of scooping down. It will sound horrible.

This opinion, shared by Rosa Burley, did not prevail: Elgar certainly did not accept Jaeger's view, nor have generations of Prom audiences since that time.

In the meantime Elgar left for Düsseldorf and the German première of *The Dream of Gerontius*. On arrival he was met by Buths, on December 16th, three days before the concert. The

The procession for the coronation of Edward VII.

basis of his fame in Germany had been already laid by performances given by Buths, and others, of the *Enigma Variations*, but *Gerontius* evoked a reaction of a far different order. It was such a success that it was selected for a second outing at the Lower Rhine Festival of 1902.

Once back in Worcestershire he settled down to two short orchestral pieces, *Dream Children;* calm, evocative and wistful, rather in the manner of the earlier *Chanson du Matin*. As Ian Parrott has written, 'If the word "imperial" is in the mind when we contemplate one side of Elgar's nature, so the word "dream" represents the other'. The word and the mood come again and again in his output, from *The Dream of Gerontius*, *Dream Children*, to the opening words of *The Music Makers* (1912);

We are the music makers, we are the dreamers of dreams.

As he grew older it was these two sides of his nature that became more and more prominent; the dreamer in works like *The Starlight Express* and the ballet *The Sanguine Fan* and the Patriot in the cluster of pieces written during the First World War.

The *Coronation Ode* was finished on 1st April 1902, ready for its first performance at a gala concert at Covent Garden on June 30th. It was not, however, destined to take place, for the day before Elgar was due to leave for London, the news came through that the King was ill and that the performance had been cancelled. Elgar's reaction to the disappointment was truly 'stiff upper lip'.

Don't for heaven's sake sympathise with me – I don't care a tinker's damn! It gives me three blessed sunny days in my own country (for which I thank God or the Devil) instead of stewing in town. *My* own interest in the thing ceased, as usual, when I had finished the M.S., since when I have been thinking mighty things! I was biking out in Herefordshire yesterday and the news reached me at a little roadside pub. I said 'Give me another pint of cider'. I'm deadly sorry for the King but that's all.

Before the anti-climax over the *Coronation Ode*, Elgar had returned to Düsseldorf for the performance of *Gerontius* at the Lower Rhine Festival in May. R.J. Buckley put the success of this performance in perspective.

Long ago Schumann said, 'English composer, no composer.' and the saying sank deep into the hearts of his countrymen, who in later years looked upon English music as meaning Arthur Sullivan and *The Mikado*. . . No English composer had been honoured at the Lower Rhine meetings since Onslow, seventy years before *Gerontius*.

After the performance at a luncheon given in Elgar's honour he received what, according to Rosa Burley, he regarded as the greatest compliment of his life. It came from Richard Strauss, whom Elgar admired more than any other living composer, who proposed the toast to 'the welfare and success of the first English progressivist, Meister Edward Elgar, and of the young progressive school of English composers'. For Elgar it meant not only the confirmation of his international status, and the acceptance of the work by English audiences and critics. Success at a foreign festival was perhaps the only thing that the home audience, dominated by an awed regard for anything Continental in the arts, accepted as reason for changing its mind. It also enhanced his self-confidence. As Rosa Burley points out:

For years he had never cut a very successful or distinguished figure on the platform. As a conductor he had been nervous, fidgety and in consequence, ill-tempered . . . And in social intercourse he had always seemed shy or awkward or, what was worse, boisterously facetious . . . Towards the end of 1902 a marked change began to set in . . . we noticed a greater assurance in his manner and a greater alertness and enthusiasm in his dealings with the choirs and orchestras which were willing to perform his works.

Richard Strauss (1864-1949).

Kramskoi's picture of Christ in the Wilderness, in the print that Elgar hung in his study at Craeg Lea.

Success also inspired him to return to large-scale composition which he had avoided since the completion of *Gerontius* two years before. Despite its luke-warm reception at the original performance, the Birmingham Festival had asked him to write another oratorio for 1903. This time he decided to be even more ambitious. Searching for a subject he remembered a remark of Francis Reeve's from his schooldays. 'The Apostles were poor men, young men, at the time of their calling; perhaps before the descent of the Holy Ghost not cleverer than some of you here.' The work, the 'mighty things' referred to in the letter above, was meant to be a trilogy of oratorios tracing the development of the Apostles' mission. For once inspiration was linked to specific places and events. For much of the material he returned to Longdon Marsh, a haunt of his boyhood, between Tewkesbury and Ledbury. W.H. Reed tells us that:

Here he used to sit and dream. A great deal of 'the Apostles' took shape in his mind there. He told me . . . he had to go there more than once to think out those climaxes in the Ascension.

Another source was an engraving, by the Russian artist Kramskoi, that hung on his study wall at Craeg Lea showing Christ, dejected and meditative, sitting hunched on a rock in the wilderness. But above all, the death of his mother in September forced him to examine the depth of his religious feeling and prompted an intensity in the music for the Apostles which, perhaps, would not have been there had the happiness of real success gone untempered. His mother had died only ten days before he was due to conduct *Gerontius* at the Worcester Festival for the first time. He had been very close to her for she had been the comforting and, through her reading and writing of poetry, the most cultured influence during his early life.

The Apostles occupied his time all through the winter of 1902 and 1903, right up until June. This at least gave the forces that were to sing at the first performance in October more time than they had been allowed for the learning of *Gerontius*. The earlier work, meanwhile, had spread Elgar's name even further afield than Germany. On 23rd March it was performed by the Apollo Music Club in Chicago, and three days later Walter Damrosch gave it for the first time in New York. In Chicago, over four thousand people had turned out to hear it, a spectacular reaction to a new work by a composer hardly known outside his own country, and one who had been recognised there for less than a decade.

The Apostles opened the Birmingham Festival on 14th October with, this time, Elgar conducting. The choir and orchestra were apparently determined not to repeat the mistakes they had made in

Gerontius or jolt their reputation further by underestimating another major new work. The result was a performance that was as impressive as the earlier one had been indifferent. The following morning *The Daily Telegraph* announced the occasion

as in some respects unique . . . for through all the years in which I have known the Birmingham Festival it has never happened that the whole musical world, not only in this country but also abroad, has gathered more or less closely round the production of an Englishman.

The newspaper's critic went on to dub the oratorio 'perhaps the most remarkable work of the present century'; fairly safe praise, considering the century was not yet four years old.

Despite the success of *The Apostles*, and his now almost universal recognition as a major composer, Elgar was unable to shake off the mood of depression caused by his mother's death. This was intensified by his inability to find the right material to make a satisfactory symphony which had long been his ambition. Furthermore, the view from Birchwood, which had been one of the greatest assets of the little cottage, was being spoilt, and the Elgars moved out for good at the end of October. However, recognition had improved his finances, if nothing else, and it was decided that the whole family, together with Rosa Burley, should spend the first part of the winter in Italy. They left for the south at the end of November and made for the little seaside town of Alassio on the Italian Riviera, between Nice and Genoa.

The first part of the holiday seems to have been a success, even though the weather was cold and damp. Elgar took the same enjoyment out of the simple elements of his new surroundings that he always did when away from England, whether it was the Midnight Mass at a little village church on Christmas Eve, or the unloading of barrels of Sicilian wine into the sea for collection. However, even in the new atmosphere of Italy he found that he could not come to grips with the symphony. Instead, as with *Gerontius* and *Cockaigne* two years earlier, he followed an oratorio with a concert overture, *In the South*. By the beginning of January the holiday had started to go sour. On the 3rd he wrote to Jaeger,

this visit has been, is, artistically a complete failure and I can do nothing: we have been perished with cold, rain and gales. Five fine days have we had and three of those were perforce spent in the train. The symphony will not be written in this sunny (?) land . . . I have never regretted anything more than this horribly disappointing journey: wasting time, money, and temper.

Consequently, when at the end of January he received an invita-

57

tion to dine with the King at Marlborough House, he was more than pleased to find an excuse to cut short the holiday and return to England.

In March 1904 London saw an event which was as extraordinary an honour for a living composer as it was unique. A three-day Elgar Festival was held at Covent Garden, performed by the Hallé Orchestra and chorus under Hans Richter. The King and Queen attended both the Monday and Tuesday performances and *In the South* was given its first outing on the last night. Sir Adrian Boult told how his friend Frank Schuster, who was also a friend of Elgar's, was instrumental in bringing about the Festival through his friendship with Henry Higgins, Chairman of the Grand Opera Syndicate. 'Lady Elgar was very tiny indeed and had a quiet, intimate way of speaking. This caused her to come close up to anyone to whom she had anything important to say. As Frank put it, "You know the way dear Alice used to come up to one and confide in one's tummy? Well, one day she said to my tummy, 'Frank, dear, we are always going to Gloucester Festivals or Leeds

ROYAL OPERA,

COVENT GARDEN.

Proprietors: THE GRAND OPERA SYNDICATE, Ltd.
Secretary & Business Manager: Mr. NEIL FORSYTH.

ELGAR FESTIVAL

The Grand Opera Syndicate, by arrangement with Mr. Alfred Schulz-Curtius, will hold a

MUSICAL FESTIVAL

consisting of the principal Works of

Dr. EDWARD ELGAR

AT

THE ROYAL OPERA, COVENT GARDEN,

ON

MONDAY, MARCH 14th, at 8 p.m.
TUESDAY, MARCH 15th, at 8 p.m.
WEDNESDAY, MARCH 16th, at 8 p.m.

The Works will be produced under the direction of

Dr HANS RICHTER

and rendered by the

HALLÉ ORCHESTRA OF 100 PERFORMERS,
THE MANCHESTER CHORUS OF 275 VOICES,

And the following Distinguished Soloists
(Named alphabetically):

Mesdames: CLARA BUTT,   Messieurs: ANDREW BLACK,
    KIRKBY LUNN,   JOHN COATES,
    AGNES NICHOLLS.   D. FFRANGCON-DAVIES,
                         KENNERLEY RUMFORD.

Dr. Hans Richter having, with his Manchester Orchestra and Chorus, devoted special attention to Dr. Elgar's Works, a perfect ensemble may be anticipated.

FOR FURTHER PARTICULARS PLEASE TURN OVER.

The Elgar Festival poster – the result of Frank Schuster's conversation with Harry Higgins of the Covent Garden Syndicate.

Festivals and so on. Don't you think we might have an Elgar Festival sometime?' My tummy reported what she had said and I went off to see Harry Higgins." '

Elgar's attitude was mixed and showed all the signs of feigned indifference that were always evident when he was not sure how to react, especially when being lavished with compliments by those he did not know or regarded as uncertain allies. Three days before the Festival Frank Schuster gave a dinner party for him. Sir Henry Wood was there and recalled that 'Elgar was in one of his very silent and stand-offish moods. In fact, his manner was so noticeable that Lady Maud Warrender, who was sitting next to me, drew my attention to it.'

'What's the matter with Elgar tonight?' she whispered. 'He seems far away from us all. I suppose it is because he doesn't like this sort of homage.'

We all felt rather uncomfortable when Schuster rose and asked us to drink the health of his illustrious friend. We obeyed, and

Elgar with his father in Polly's garden at Stoke, taken by Polly's daughter, May, on 23rd May 1904.

when we resumed our seats we naturally expected Elgar to make a suitable reply. Instead he went on talking to an old friend and probably had no idea his health had been drunk at all.'

The whole week was a continuous round of parties and receptions. They were presented on the second night to the King and Queen ('Mrs. E . . . must have been in the 7th heaven of happiness. Such swells they met from the Queen downwards', Jaeger wrote to Dora Penny) and at Lord Northampton's house they were introduced to the Prime Minister, Arthur Balfour.

At the end of April Elgar heard that he had been elected to the Athenaeum, and in May he returned to Germany to hear Fritz Steinbach conduct *The Apostles* at Cologne, returning by way of Düsseldorf to see Julius Buths, and reaching England again by the end of the month. The University of Durham decided to give Elgar an honorary Doctorate of Music, and while he was away a letter from the Prime Minister arrived informing him that he was to receive a knighthood. The day after his return Elgar cycled over to tell his father at Stoke, a moment which his niece photographed.

On July 5th he went to Buckingham Palace. He was now, as Sir Edward Elgar, not only recognised as a musician and the most important English composer at home and on the Continent, but he was also a public figure and firmly a member of the cultural establishment, made welcome by the aristocratic class. Only five years before he had been an obscure composer for the provincial festival circuit. He was forty-seven at the time of knighthood. If it had taken a long time to convince the world that he was a serious composer, once the momentum of fame was started it gathered pace remarkably fast.

4　Mature Symphonist

The King conferred the new knighthood on July 5th at Buckingham Palace. 'Very pleased to see you here, Sir Edward,' he said, 'Good sport to your fishing.' Four days earlier the Elgars had finally moved from 'Craeg Lea' in Malvern, to Hereford. Their house was almost the last building of the town, on the road to the village of Mordiford. 'Plas Gwyn' is large and airy, with a covered verandah running round three sides overlooking the River Wye, only a few yards away. Although Elgar's finances were little better (he complained to Jaeger the following month that the *Enigma Variations*, performed from New York to St. Petersburg, had earned him only eight pounds in five years) the size of the house did reflect his new knightly station, a point of importance to Lady Elgar. But above all, he now had a really spacious study with plenty of space for bookcases and his piano, as well as a large mahogany table capable of taking an expanse of manuscript paper, standing in the middle of the room.

The summer was spent settling in. Although 'Plas Gwyn' did not have the advantages of the Malvern Hills or of Birchwood's trees, it was at least easier cycling country. Proof correcting for Novellos took up a lot of time and he also worked on the sketches for the second of his biblical oratorios. This eventually became *The Kingdom*, but at that stage it was referred to simply as Part II of *The Apostles*. Another honorary degree was presented by Leeds University during the festival in October. This time it was an LL.D., a qualification that one year's tenure of the post of office boy in a law firm hardly prepared him for. However his graduation into the legal profession can at least be said to have been painless. The second performance of *In the South* was also given at Leeds – a compromise result of a series of misunderstandings which had started with the festival committee expecting first an oratorio, then a symphony and, having failed to get either, excluding Elgar's music from the event altogether. It was only Stanford's

Plas Gwyn, Hereford.

insistence, as Festival Conductor, that restored him to the prog-ramme. Despite Stanford's previous championship (he had been one of the first to recognise Elgar as a major voice in English music and it had been at his suggestion that Cambridge had been the first to award him an honorary doctorate) it was virtually the last time the two composers met amicably. In December it seems that Stanford wrote Elgar an unpleasant letter ('odious' was the word Alice used). It has not survived, but it must have amounted to a personal attack, for they remained on frosty terms for the rest of their lives and definitely hostile for twenty years. It is possible it had something to do with the campaign for an adequate copyright law for which Stanford was working hard. He felt that leaders of the profession were not doing as much as they might to support his campaign, though in fairness Elgar had given a speech on the subject the day before he received his knighthood. Whatever the cause it was a squabble that brought out the most childishly sensitive part of Elgar's nature and widened still further the breach between him and London's music colleges – Stanford being prin-cipal of the Royal College of Music.

The academic world, however, was about to involve him deeply in its affairs. Richard Peyton, a wealthy benefactor of Midland arts, offered to contribute £10,000 to the endowment of a Chair of Music at the new University of Birmingham. His only condition was that it should be offered to Elgar and accepted by him as the first Professor. This put Elgar in something of a cleft stick. He had been connected with the cultural life of the city ever since his days as a rank-and-file violinist in Stockley's orchestra. Many of his works had received their first performances there. He was as much a part of Birmingham as he was of Worcester and so was the obvious person for the job. At the same time, he was understand-ably nervous about a post which would inevitably attract public attention and for which, having no contact with further education at all, he felt himself completely unfitted. There was the possibil-ity that it would be like teaching (which he regarded as 'like turning a grindstone with a dislocated shoulder') and was con-vinced, in the event with considerable justification, that all the battalions of the establishment would be arrayed against him and his lectures. However he did not want to deprive the University of its professorship and, besides, there was plenty he wanted to say. After much thought he accepted, but on the condition that he could resign after three years if he felt the post was not satisfactory. The appointment was to prove every bit as controversial as he had feared, although much of value was done and the musical world was as stirred up as he could have wished. But the strain of the lectures badly affected his health during the whole period. Like so much else in his life, he took the responsibilities and the criticism that resulted far too seriously, and dropped into the spasms of nervous depression that were as exhausting for his family, and friends as they were creatively productive.

Once the decision to accept the Chair had been taken the Elgars left on their second journey of the year to Germany. They heard *The Apostles* twice, once in Mainz in a triumphant performance conducted by Fritz Volbach, and again in Rotterdam. They took the opportunity of calling on Buths in Düsseldorf, on their way to hear Steinbach's rendering of *In the South* in Cologne.

Perhaps the most exciting and significant event in English musical circles in 1904 was the founding of the London Symphony Orchestra, for which Henry Wood was largely responsible. He finally lost all patience with the system by which orchestral players were allowed to appoint unapproved deputies at rehearsals, or even at actual concerts. It was quite common for the conductor to find a substantially different section facing him at the concert from the one at the morning's rehearsal.

One morning at the Queen's Hall Robert Newman, the manager of the Promenade Concerts, advanced onto the platform and announced Wood's decree;

Gentlemen, in future there will be no deputies. Good Morning!

Half the orchestra immediately walked out. These players formed themselves into the country's first self-governing orchestra, with powers to appoint and fire their conductors. The new body also departed from the then accepted rule in London by not being tied to a particular Hall or management. It was soon recognised as one of the country's finest ensembles and Richter, Steinbach and Elgar all eagerly conducted the new orchestra in the early years.

In October Jaeger saw the opportunity of combining Elgar's growing commitment to instrumental writing with the launch of the LSO.

I hope you can write the Symphony Orchestra a short new work. Why not a *brilliant* quick String Scherzo, or something for those fine strings only? a real bring the house down *torrent* of a thing as Bach could write . . . It wouldn't take you away from your big work for long. You might even write a *modern Fugue* . . .

Elgar mulled over the idea while on the Continent, and was hard at work on it at 'Plas Gwyn' throughout January. By 26th he was able to report back to a sick Jaeger, now trying to recover in the Swiss resort of Davos,

I'm doing that string thing in time for the Sym. Orch. concert. Intro: &

Allegro – no *working-out* part but a devil of a fugue instead. G major & the sd. divvel in G minor with all sorts of japes and counterpoint.

Less than a month later it was finished;

. . . it's all right; of course it will take you sometime to get used to it, but it will sound really wholesome & bring out much tone from the strings.

Progress had been interrupted briefly by the conferment of another honorary doctorate, this time for music, from Oxford, where Sir Hubert Parry made an appreciative speech. There was never the same antagonism between Parry and Elgar as that which existed between Elgar and Stanford. For one thing they shared the same interests: Parry was as much part of the Gloucestershire countryside as Elgar was of Worcestershire, and he went out of his way in his lectures not to criticise Parry's music.

The *Introduction and Allegro for Strings* was first performed only three weeks after its completion. Elgar conducted at the Queen's Hall a concert which also included the *Enigma Variations* and the incidental music for *Grania and Diarmid*. The third *Pomp and Circumstance March*, written the previous Autumn, also received its first performance. It was the *Introduction and Allegro*, however, which caught the attention: 'many people think it the finest thing he has written', Alice wrote. Certainly the haunting theme that is first heard from the solo quartet in the Introduction and the Coda is one of the most evocative that he ever invented. As he explained in the programme note, its genesis had been found in a moment wandering along the sea shore during his Welsh holiday in 1901.

On the cliff, between blue sea and blue sky, thinking out my theme, there came up to me the sound of singing. The songs were too far away to reach me distinctly, but one point common to all was pressed upon me, and led me to think, perhaps wrongly, that it was a real Welsh idiom – I mean the fall of a third.

He had noted a snatch and labelled it 'Ynys Lochtyn.'

The sketch was forgotten until a short time ago, when it was brought to mind by hearing, far down our own Valley of the Wye a song similar to those . . . 'All the waters in Wye cannot wash the Welsh blood out of its body' – the work is really a tribute to that sweet borderland where I have made my home.

The dedication of this most British of works is to an American, Professor Sanford of Yale, who had invited Elgar to visit the university that June to receive yet another doctorate.

Despite the success of the new pieces, it was the thought of his inaugural lecture at Birmingham which really occupied him. The nearer the ordeal, the more apprehensive he became. In the event, whatever his private misgivings, he carried the day with his usual public aplomb. Frank Schuster and Alfred Kalisch, a friendly critic, accompanied him from London to give moral support and, dressed in his Cambridge robes, he entered the crowded hall of the Midland Institute together with the University's Principal, Sir Oliver Lodge, while selections from his music were played on the organ.

The eight lectures he gave over the course of the next two years make intriguing reading, for they show not only how deeply and passionately he thought and felt about his subjects, but also where his prejudices lay. In general his observations were accurate, often uncomfortably so for some people, and his pleas for public and municipal support for the arts prophetic. The first lecture, 'A Future for English Music', was seen as, and indeed was, an attack on the mediocrity of the Establishment, in particular its complete

Sir Oliver Lodge, spiritualist, scientist and principal of Birmingham University while Elgar was Professor of Music.

lack of invention. Parts of the lecture are well worth quoting, if only to show why Elgar, despite his knighthood and with a now almost unassailable reputation, was still regarded as something of an 'enfant terrible':-

Some of us who in that year (1880) were young and taking an active part in music – a really active part such as playing in orchestras – felt that something at last was going to be done in the way of composition by the English school . . . Some of us who were accustomed to play the works of Beethoven, Weber . . . and Wagner – while anxious to believe all that a friendly Press told us about the glories of the new English school, could not help feeling that the music given us to play was, not to put too fine a point on it, rather dry . . . the greater portion [is] dead and forgotten and only exist[s] as [a] warning to the student of the twentieth century. It is saddening to those who hoped so much from these early days, to find that after all that had been written, and all the endeavour to excite enthusiasm for English music . . . that he had inherited an art which has no hold on the affections of our own people, and is held in no respect abroad . . . The art that stands still is dead; the art that moves, or I would say progresses, is alive . . . More difficult to deal with are . . . the men who go about assuming that they are most modern and singing revolutionary songs to the wrong tune. It is all very well to sing 'Ca ira, Ca ira' but the effect is quite lost if it is chanted to the Old Hundredth, and excites nothing but pity for the performer . . . Dr. Richard Strauss in a vivid speech made at Düsseldorf [after the Lower Rhine Festival performance of *Gerontius*] three or four years back, threw a brilliant illumination on this somewhat darkened picture. We all knew, although we dared not say so in so many words, what he then told us: that Arne was somewhat less than Handel; that Sterndale Bennett was some-what less than Mendelssohn, and that some Englishmen of later day were not quite so great as Brahms . . . The words to some had a bitter taste, but if the actual words were rue, the inferences drawn were hem-lock . . . Critics frequently say of a man that it is to his credit that he is never vulgar. Good. But it is possible for him . . . to be much worse; he can be commonplace . . . Vulgarity often goes with inventiveness, and it can take the initiative – in a rude and misguided way no doubt – but after all it does something, and can be and has been refined. But the common-place mind can never be anything but commonplace, and no amount of education, no polish of a university, can eradicate the stain from the low type of mind which is the English commonplace . . . An Englishman will take you into a large room, beautifully proportioned and will point out to you that it is white – all over white – and somebody will say what exquisite taste. You know in your own mind, in your own soul, that it is not taste at all – that it is want of taste – that it is mere evasion. English music is white, and evades everything.

It is a pity that after so much good sense and very courageous stand for honesty, Elgar then showed himself a victim of exactly the sort of narrow-mindedness that he was attacking:

More pitiful than anything that I have mentioned up to the present moment, are the anaemic followers of the modern French school. Their numbers are happily few, and their influence nil; but the younger generation is never more irritating than when it apes a sickly sentimentality such as we find in the decadence of the modern French School.

So much for Debussy and, by association, Elgar's friend Fauré. This attitude goes a long way to explaining why so many of the 'younger generation', excited by the harmonic innovations of the French composers, noticeably distanced themselves from Elgar's music. The fact that the three most important figures amongst them, Frank Bridge, John Ireland and Vaughan Williams, who studied for a time with Ravel, were all pupils of the estranged Stanford did not help to endear Elgar to them.

Elgar went on to say exactly how he did want music to develop:-

There are many possible futures. But the one I want to see coming into being is something that shall grow out of our own soil, something broad, noble, chivalrous, healthy and above all, an out-of-door spirit. To arrive at this it will be necessary to throw over all imitation.

Given these sentiments it is surprising that he was so indifferent to the revival in English folk-song then blossoming, which, involving long walks for Cecil Sharp, Vaughan Williams, Holst, Grainger and others, could not have been more involved either with the nation's heritage or the out-of-doors. Presumably he regarded it as just a novel form of imitation. He finished his first-ever lecture with a final slash at the prevalent atmosphere of self-congratulation:

The world revolves and the great things still go on, and the little clique is nothing more than a kitten playing with its own tail. You students have something – or should have – a higher ideal altogether.

It was not long after Elgar had dined again with the King at Buckingham Palace that the storm was unleashed. The April issue of *Musical Opinion* spoke of 'thunderbolts ready to be launched from South Kensington and Tenterden Street' (The Royal College and Royal Academy of Music). The same article made one of the most often-repeated but relevant points about Elgar:

his education and early environment have done much for him. He has never been the centre of a mutual admiration society; and, above all, he has not had to grind out the most creative years of his life as a professor or as head of a teaching institution. I verily believe that the Royal College and Royal Academy of Music have been the death of the creative life of Parry, Stanford and Mackenzie.

Frank Schuster with Elgar at the Hut. It was here that the composer found the peace and friendly atmosphere he needed to complete his major works in the first decade of the century.

It was exactly this trap of a suffocating daily routine that his friends were anxious that he should avoid and, indeed, it was another reason why he was so reluctant to take up the offer of the professorship. In fact, as often happened, the emotional trial and struggle spurred him on to greater creativity, rather than less. His period at the University saw the composition of some of his finest work in *The Kingdom* and, at last, the First Symphony. Strangely, considering his debilitated state of health and almost constant depression, both these and the *Wand of Youth Suites*, which he reworked from his teenage music for wind quintet, are dominated by zealous optimism.

Such optimism needed time to work through his system, however, and the *Introduction and Allegro* remained the only major work of 1905.

In June the Elgars sailed to America for the first time to collect the promised honorary Mus.D. from Professor Sanford at Yale. Much as he liked Sanford, and although he had several American friends, he never felt at home in America and was glad, after a month in Boston, to start the voyage home from New York on July 11th. The heat was his main complaint.

For the rest of the summer he was able to relax in his garden by the Wye and enjoy the hospitality of his friends: not so much now the genteel gatherings of country gentry, but the dinner parties of the aristocracy with Alice revelling in the high society. Lady Maud Warrender, Lord Northampton and Lord Howe were all friends, while Edward became a regular feature on the guest lists of such wealthy patrons of the arts as Frank Schuster and Edward Speyer.

The Three Choirs Festival of 1905 was for Elgar the most splendid yet. During the week both *The Dream of Gerontius* and *The Apostles*, as well as the *Introduction and Allegro*, were performed. This unprecedented representation was put in the shade, though, by a ceremony at Worcester Guildhall when, at the instigation of the new Lord Mayor – his friend since boyhood, Hubert Leicester – Elgar was made an Honorary Freeman of the City, the highest honour the Council could bestow. After the ceremony, for which Elgar wore his new robes from Yale, the civic dignitaries processed down the High Street to the Cathedral for a performance of *Gerontius*. As they passed Elgar Bros. the composer lifted his cap in salute to his father who, at the age of eighty-three, was too ill to attend but sat watching from the upstairs window of his shop.

Elgar was still not well, however, and was worried about the continuation of his lecture series which he had agreed to give in November. With characteristic generosity Frank Schuster suggested that he should arrange a cruise around the Mediterranean, and September and the early part of October were spent, without the rest of the family, investigating southern ports. The weather

Elgar receives the Freedom of the City of Worcester, 12th September 1905. With him is the mayor, his school friend and member of the boyhood wind quintet, Hubert Leicester.

was much kinder to him than it had been on his visit to Alassio the year before, and the cruise was a considerable success. But once it was over, the lectures had to be faced.

Before the end of the year he gave talks, all well attended by the press as well as the public, on English Composers, Brahms' Symphony No. 3, English Executants and Critics. This latter was not an attack on those who had written about him, as might have been expected, but a sensible appraisal of critical problems: the unfortunate necessity of rushed journalistic notices for the daily papers; praise for Bennet of *The Daily Telegraph* and Arthur Johnstone, dead by then, of the *Manchester Guardian*, also Vernon Blackburn and Tovey. It was the lecture on Brahms which caused the most argument, or rather, one passage in which he referred to absolute music (i.e. music without a literary or programmatic base) as the highest form of art. This provoked a protesting article and an answer from two of the greatest critics of *The Manchester Guardian*, Ernest Newman and Samuel Langford. Newman's observation that Elgar was not only dismissing most of his own music but, amongst others, a fair amount of Beethoven was met by Langford with a characteristically beautiful passage of writing.

It is the distinction of music that it alone among the arts is primarily an expression of transcendental feeling, the feeling which accompanies us through all our experiences . . . it is born free and unfettered, and so it is a 'simple' art in a sense that other arts are not, and can be 'at its height' without description.

Elgar reiterated the point in his final lecture of the series, Retrospect, given on December 13th:

I still look upon music which exists without any poetic or literary basis as the true foundation of our art . . . I HAVE written overtures with titles more or less poetic or suggestive: am I then so narrow as to admire my own music because I have written it myself? Certainly not . . . Let me say definitely that when I see one of my own works by the side of, say, the Fifth Symphony, I feel like a tinker may do when surveying the Forth Bridge . . .

Newman's astonishment at Elgar's rejection of programme music is not surprising for, up to this date, he had written nothing important, except the *Serenade for Strings*, which did not have some sort of external point of reference. However Elgar's attitude was changing rapidly, and though he was then engaged mainly on the completion of *The Kingdom* it was the thought of a symphony, and the germ of an idea for a violin concerto, that he was really exploring. In fact, although there were to be plenty more descriptive pieces, *The Music Makers* stands alone as a 'non-absolute' creation amongst the major works of his last fifteen years of important activity.

In between the lectures he went on a long and varyingly successful tour conducting the London Symphony Orchestra, starting in Birmingham the night after his lecture on Brahms' third symphony, which formed the corner stone of his programme. Liverpool, Manchester, Bradford, Sheffield, Newcastle and even Glasgow were visited. The orchestra, on its first tour outside London, aroused great interest but mixed notices: the provincial critics felt that a selection from Brahms, Dvorak, Mozart and Elgar was far too advanced for the majority of its conservative audiences!

At home in Hereford the sketches for *The Kingdom*, mostly jotted down at the same time as work for *The Apostles*, had to be gathered into shape ready for the Birmingham Festival of 1906. Composing, as he had feared, had been neglected during the first year as a professor and it needed an intense period of work to catch up. Dora Penny, who visited the Elgars at the end of the year, left a revealing account of life in the household and Alice's lonely evenings when major work was in progress. He had been working all day and emerged for dinner:–

He never spoke. When he was not looking at his plate he looked straight in front of him with a rather tense expression. He was very pale and looked tired and drawn. Half-way through dessert he pushed his chair back, hit my hand, which happened to be on the table, quite sharply, and left the room. He banged the study door and turned the key . . . When 10.30 came the Lady said . . . 'Don't you think it would be nice to make ourselves some tea?' I went with her to the kitchen, and there was a tea-tray all put ready and a large plate of sandwiches covered over . . . We had two sandwiches each and took all the rest to the tray on the

Elgar sits at his desk working at a full score in 1909. May Grafton, his niece, took the picture.

oak chest. While we were drinking our tea we heard the piano at last . . . I don't know how long he went on playing, but silence came at length and we both realised it must be very late and that we were greatly in need of another brew of tea. I went out and made it this time and the hall clock struck half-past one as I passed it . . . We heard his key turn and the Lady got up and opened the drawing-room door. 'Hullo! You still up? and Dorabella too? and tea! Oh, my giddy aunt! This is good! . . . Then he played the whole of that evening's work, and more, straight through . . . '

Even composers can't function in England without liberal quantities of tea!

He worked steadily through the early months of the new year but for once his heart did not seem to be in the project, and it was plainly a struggle. He was given some encouragement in March when Alfred Littleton, head of Novellos, came to see him. Much impressed, Littleton suggested the title for the new work but by April, when Elgar left for a second visit to America, there was still much to be done. He had tentatively asked the Birmingham Festival committee whether they would accept half an oratorio. While in America a further blow to his will to compose came in a telegram announcing the death of his father, and one wonders how much interest he took in his conducting engagements at the Cincinnati Festival. When he returned, Alice took him to Wales to recover, but it was not until he reached Frank Schuster's house by the Thames, near Maidenhead, in July, that he felt able to settle to serious work on *The Kingdom* again.

'The Hut', as Schuster called his riverside mansion, was equipped as an ideal retreat for artistic endeavour of all kinds. Here Elgar could work in peace and yet know that his most sympathetic friends were around him to give encouragement, play through his work, or to join him on fishing expeditions. The rest at Bray did the trick and by August, back at home in Hereford, he was writing and scoring the music faster than he had ever done, ignoring the proceedings of the Three Choirs Festival at the Cathedral and not even bothering to attend *Gerontius*. He was, no doubt, anxious that history should not repeat itself and leave him with an under-rehearsed choir suspicious of a new work.

In the event he need not have worried. By now the orchestral players were sympathetic to his music and the chorus, trained by the dedicated R.H. Wilson, could this time be relied on to give of their best. Ten days before the first performance of *The Kingdom* on October 3rd he travelled to Aberdeen to accept an LL.D. from the University (his first from Scotland). Even though he had written to Jaeger, 'the whole thing is intentionally less mystic than the A(postles):- the men are alive and working and the atmosphere is meant to be more direct and simple', *The Kingdom* moved him deeply and he was to be seen weeping several times as he conducted it. In spite of the enthusiastic success the work received, the emotional strain was too great and he admitted, in his usual state of melancholy following a major première, that he would not write another oratorio, or even complete the third part of the trilogy, though much of it was already sketched.

To add to his gloom, the time for lecturing was again approaching. For his final two topics he chose Orchestration and Mozart's *G minor Symphony (No. 40: K.550)*, which he had used as his model for his symphonic exercise as a boy. Orchestration was the one department of music in which Elgar can safely be said to have had no peer. His writing for choirs, solo voice, the organ and, on rare occasions (for he disliked the instrument), the piano, was capable and thoughtful, but the orchestra was his natural medium and his music came to him already clothed in orchestral colours. As he made clear in his lecture:–

Orchestration in its highest sense is the art of composing for an orchestra: NOT the perfunctory matter of ARRANGING ideas for instruments . . . I find it impossible to imagine a composer creating a musical idea without defining inwardly, and simultaneously, the exact means of its presentation . . . But what are we to say of those who approach the orchestra through the piano? No two things could be more dissimilar; they only resemble each other in so far as both are capable of complete harmony and not, as in a single violin for instance, an extremely limited range of chords . . . Now the rigid piano is capable of only . . . four distinct weights of tone. Beyond this the piano cannot go. The modern orchestra is capable of an unending variety of shades of tone, not only in succession, but in combination . . . harmonies which may sound execrable and impossible on the piano . . . may give the greatest pleasure when scored for instruments.

As has been seen in Dora Penny's account of the composition of *The Kingdom*, above, Elgar only used the piano at the end of the process to play through what he had already written with the orchestra in mind. In the same lecture he said 'We have only touched on the fringes of the possibilities of modern harmony.', a statement that partly redresses the balance of his earlier remarks about modern French composers.

With the lectures thankfully disposed of he felt much relieved, but exhausted by the twin exertions of *The Kingdom* and his university commitments. The Elgars therefore decided that a lengthy change of surroundings was necessary. They went first across the border to Wales, and once on the move he did not return to England for any length of time for several months. January and February 1907 were spent in Italy and at the beginning of March he left on his own for New York, where he conducted performances both of *The Apostles* and *The Kingdom*, as well as travelling to Chicago and Pittsburgh for the *Enigma Variations* and yet another academic honour. He had, he wrote to Jaeger on his return, 'a mixed time in America – mostly very pleasant but the unpleasant times were jokable, so all passed well.'

Established once more at 'Plas Gwyn' in May he produced the *Pomp and Circumstance No. 4*, perhaps in a surge of patriotism not uncommon when one comes home after four months abroad. It was dedicated to G.R. Sinclair of Hereford Cathedral (the eleventh of the Variations): something for him personally this time, rather than for his dog! While Elgar had been in the United States his wife had taken the matter of the Professorship into her own hands, and had gone to the authorities to suggest that instead of having to give lectures himself, Elgar should merely arrange the series. This the University agreed to. Since everything Elgar had said had raised a massive controversy in the press they were probably as relieved as he was, having delivered a none too subtle hint of their discomfort by accommodating his Mozart talk in a small room too cramped to hold all those who wanted to attend. So in 1907 the lectures were delivered by his fellow composer Walford Davies, the American academic Thomas Surette and the critic Ernest Newman. Elgar attended only the first two lectures, and the following summer he resigned.

Another landmark in his life, which he was eager to forget, was due on June 2nd. He wrote to Jaeger, who was struggling with illness once again and trying to escape the consequences of tuberculosis by convalescence in Germany.

I shall be fifty next week so they tell me, but I don't know it. I have my pipe & the bicycle & heavenly country to ride in – so an end. I take no interest whatever in music now & just 'edit' a few old boyish M.S.S. – music is off.

The 'boyish M.S.S.' were the books of sketches saved from his childhood. Now, when he was not fishing or building a hutch for Carice's rabbit, he worked on them and eventually produced *The Wand of Youth Suite (No. 1)*.

Far more importantly he had begun to sketch not only a symphony, but also the violin concerto and a string quartet; his first attempt at the form since his discarded juvenilia of the 1880s. Late in June he had played his family the theme which was to become the great 'nobilmente' opening of the First Symphony, and the ideas progressed steadily throughout the rest of the year. It was decided to winter once more in Italy and so at the beginning of

November they left for Rome. There, at first, the work moved forward and much of the first movement emerged. Gradually, though, the music stopped. He was thoroughly happy in the sun and among the ancient sights, and the six months in the south were this time spent pleasurably but unproductively, except for a joint musical Christmas card, 'A Christmas Greeting' (words by Alice), which was sent rather at the last minute to Sinclair for the choristers at Hereford to sing. It was not until May, when they left their rooms in the Via Gregoriana and returned to 'Plas Gwyn', that he pushed ahead with any facility. As he complained to Jaeger, part of the problem was noise:

I cannot afford to get a *quiet* studio where I might have worked & my whole winter has been wasted for the want of a few more pounds . . . I resent it bitterly but can do nothing. It is just the same now at Hereford, noise has developed in the neighbourhood – I dodged it doing *The Kingdom* at great expense by going to Wales, but I can't do it again: my lovely works do not pay the rent of a studio!

Between 'Plas Gwyn' and the river is a road, not a big one by modern standards, that leads to Mordiford. Elgar was experiencing the first irritating intrusion of the motor car, which also disturbed his cycling.

Once home, despite a crusty note to Jaeger ('I have no intention of completing my oratorio cycle or whatever it is . . . Of course I have the thing – the biggest of all sketched – but I cannot afford for the sake of others to waste any time on it.'), he found that ideas were flowing into a big work for the first time in two years. 'I can't answer your letter at this moment. I can't say I have anything more important to do but it must be done and done now. Oh! such a tune.' he wrote on June 13th. All through the summer of 1908 he was writing fast, and a visit to Schuster in July spurred him on, as it had done with *The Kingdom*. By the time it was orchestrated and he was finally satisfied, on September 25th, he was exhausted. But the symphony, which had nagged him for almost a decade, ever since a work about General Gordon had been suggested after the composition of the *Variations*, was at last written. It had taken him eleven years longer than Brahms to find the confidence to put his first symphonic thoughts down on paper and, by way of decisive answer to Newman's comments on his lecture three years before, it was his first large scale piece of abstract music. That it took him so long is, surely, not only a reflection on his own insecurity but on that of English music in general. Before the appearance of the A flat symphony there had been little comparable and nothing as accomplished. English music, it seems, did not have the confidence to produce a composer prepared to meet the great

European tradition of symphonic thought on its own terms, preferring instead to languish in the backwaters of oratorio, overtures and insipid cantata. Even *Enigma* and Parry's *Symphonic Variations* (interestingly enough, written the year before Elgar's) were only half measures towards dealing with the awesome ghost of Brahms. Within a year of Elgar England's other great symphonist, Ralph Vaughan Williams, had introduced his 1st Symphony, *The Sea*, at the Leeds Festival.

In November Hans Richter came to stay at 'Plas Gwyn' to look through the work which was dedicated to him – 'True artist and True Friend'. Richter was an invaluable champion of Elgar's work, partly because of his immense international reputation, having been entrusted with first performances by both Wagner and Brahms, but mainly because be believed unreservedly in the greatness of Elgar's music. On one occasion in Manchester, when he conducted the *Introduction and Allegro* for the first time, the

The 1st page of the First Symphony. Notice the typical Elgarian tempo marking, 'nobilmente'. (Novello & Co.)

audience's reaction was polite but no more. They evidently had not understood it, so Richter played it again! With Elgar he felt he had to make a special effort, for he never forgave himself for the fiasco of the first performance of *Gerontius*.

Manchester was the first city to hear the *Symphony*, on December 3rd, at a Hallé Orchestra concert conducted by Richter. It was an immediate and overwhelming success, with Elgar and the players having to acknowledge the applause after the slow movement. In London, four days later, Richter's performance with the London Symphony Orchestra was greeted by a standing ovation. Jaeger, by now obviously dying, forced himself to the Queen's Hall. Three days before he wrote to his friend the last letter that survives:

It's a great and masterly work & will place you higher among the world's masters than anything you have done.' After the concert he wrote to Dora Penny: 'I never in all my experience saw the like. The hall was packed; any amount of musicians . . . After the first movement E.E. was called out, again, several times after the third and then came the great moment. After that superb Coda the audience seemed to rise at E. when he appeared. I *never* heard such frantic applause . . . people stood up and even *on* their seats to get a view.

To Richter it was 'the greatest symphony of modern times, and not only in this country'. In the year following its first performance in Manchester the Symphony No. 1 was given in Vienna, Leipzig, Berlin, Bonn, Boston, Sydney, St. Petersburg and New York, (where Walter Damrosch gave the first American performance on 3rd January 1909, only a month after its première,) as well as on seventeen occasions in London. Every English conductor took it into his repertory: Wood, Landon Ronald and Thomas Beecham all contributed to the extraordinary total of eighty-two performances in one year. No other work by an Englishman had ever been acclaimed so widely, so fast. The great critic Neville Cardus, writing in 1945, explained the reason for such a manic show of exhilaration over this new piece of music:

No English symphony existed then, at least not big enough to . . . go in the programme of a concert side by side with the acknowledged masterpieces, and not be dwarfed at once into insignificance . . . I cannot hope, at this time of day, to describe the pride taken in Elgar by young English students of that far-away epoch.

For Elgar personally the success put him irrevocably at the head of his profession but, true to form, he could not resist at least a semblance of indifference. He wrote to Adela Schuster, Frank's sister, on Christmas Day.

Elgar concocting one of his less explosive substances in 'the Ark', a shed he converted at the back of Plas Gwyn.

I receive heaps of letters from persons known and unknown telling me how it uplifts them: I wish it uplifted me – I have just paid rent, Land Tax, Income Tax & a variety of other things due today and there are children yapping at the door. 'Christians awake! Salute the "yappy" morn'. I saluted it about seven o'clock, quite dark, made a fire in the Ark & mused on the future of a bad cold in my head.

'The Ark' was the centre of Elgar's absorbing, and now and again dangerous, interest in chemistry. He converted a shed at the back of 'Plas Gwyn' into a fully equipped laboratory and was completely happy when mixing or inventing. It was really an extension of a boy's passion for chemistry sets, but he was intensely proud when his machine for producing sulphurated hydrogen was patented and produced as the 'Elgar S.H. Apparatus'. That the hobby could prove explosive is related by W.H. Reed:

One day he made a phosphoric concoction which, when dry, would 'go off' by spontaneous combustion. The amusement was to smear it on a piece of blotting paper and then wait breathlessly for the catastrophe. One day he made too much paste; . . . he clapped the whole of it into a gallipot, covered it up, and dumped it into the water-butt, thinking it would be safe there. Just as he was getting on famously . . . a sudden unexpected crash . . . shook the room . . . The water-butt had blown-up: the hoops were rent: the staves flew in all directions; and the liberated water went down the drive in a solid wall. Silence reigned for a few seconds. Then all the dogs in Herefordshire gave tongue . . . After a moment's thought, Edward lit his pipe and strolled down to the gate, andante tranquillo, as if nothing had happened . . . A neighbour, peeping out of his gate, called out, 'Did you hear that noise, sir: it sounded like an explosion?' 'Yes', said Sir Edward. 'I heard it; where was it?'

Reed, the leader of the LSO, was to become more and more a feature of Elgar's life, for old friends were passing. Jaeger finally succumbed to his long illness in May and Basil Nevinson and William Grafton, his brother-in-law, also died at this time. Jaeger's death was a blow not only for Elgar but for the whole of English music, as was shown by the memorial concert at the Queen's Hall on 24th January 1910 when the London Symphony Orchestra was conducted by Coleridge-Taylor, Walford Davies and Parry in their own works, while Richter contributed some Wagner, Brahm's *Alto Rhapsody* and appropriate parts of the *Enigma Variations*. A remarkable tribute to a publishing editor.

But despite such losses Elgar was in excellent spirits. In April, having done no work during the winter, he went again to Italy, stopping in Paris for a few days exploring on his own before the family arrived. This time they based themselves at Caraggi; near Florence, where they were put up in a villa belonging to Mrs. Julia Worthington. 'Pippa' was a valued companion, whom they had met in New York four years before. She was wealthy and her marriage was not a success, and she naturally attached herself to the Elgars. In Rome, on the previous visit, she and Edward had made several trips to the theatre together. Rosa Burley, who had departed rather abruptly for Portugal when the finances of 'The Mount' had collapsed in 1906, joined them for a while. From Florence they took a leisurely way home, meandering through the north of Italy from Pisa, Bologna (leaving Carice for the moment with Pippa) to Venice where ideas for a violin concerto started to take coherent shape. Inspired by St. Mark's he wrote two part-songs, *Go, Song of Mine* and *The Angelus*. Old haunts at Garmisch were revisited, the excuse being to visit Strauss who now lived there. As well as the concerto there were now also the beginnings in his mind of another symphony jotted down in his sketchbooks.

5 Established in London

This last Edwardian summer was almost perfect. The first rumblings of international tension did not penetrate the peace of Herefordshire or Maidenhead. Elgar was at the height of his fame and of his creative powers. He had the recognition it had once seemed impossible that he would ever achieve, a reputation not only of national but of world stature. Now, if ever, the wish he had confided to his mother many years before might have been fulfilled. He could not, he had told her, be content until he received a letter from abroad addressed to Edward Elgar, England. He could afford for the time being to rest securely on his laurels, so very little was done that summer. A fine evening, after the garden had been watered, was spent playing the sketches for the violin concerto on the piano through the open window to Dorabella and Alice on the lawn. For the Hereford Festival another house was rented for a large house party (Carice having inconveniently contracted scarlet fever) which included Julia Worthington and Frank Schuster, as well as Professor Sanford Terry from Aberdeen and Nicholas Kilburn and his wife, his early champions from Bishop Auckland. The party found Elgar in high spirits and completely in charge, his wife having to remain in quarantine with Carice, who was able to talk to friends over the garden gate. Amongst the lively fringe events was Elgar's private concert, a selection from the programme of which gives a good idea of its aesthetic aspirations!

1910 was an unsettled year for the country with two general elections, the limitation of the powers of the House of Lords, the death of King Edward VII, as well as the continued calls for industrial and social change which had brought the Liberals into power decisively in 1905. Nevertheless, it was an excellent year for Elgar: he was now indisputedly a public figure. The *Violin Concerto*, on which he restarted serious work early in the new year, was composed not only in the peace of Herefordshire but during social visits to country houses or in between engagements in London. In

Grand Culminating Cataclysmic
CONCERT & FIREWORK JERKATION
PROGRAMME (W.P.)

'ympanocrastic Detonation of a Brass Bombardon 'an Delian
elphone.

Beware of Pick-pockets!

verture 'I Diavoli deliriosi'   Sans-Sens (Op. 2⁵/₄A)

ORCHESTRA

gs	None
Wind (the blooming lot)	Mr. L.F. Schuster
pet	Sir E.J. Solomon Elgar
rious Horn	Mr. C.S. Terry
ssion	Mrs. Worthington & Mr. N. Kilburn
pal Solo Bagpipe	Mrs. N. Kilburn
Piano	A Chair.

Elgar's private Concert programme for the Three Choirs Festival, 1910.

79

Musical Knights in 1910: The Bournemouth Centenary Festival. Standing: Edward German, Hubert Parry. Sitting: Elgar, Dan Godfrey (the founder and conductor of the Bournemouth Symphony Orchestra), Alexander Mackenzie and Charles Stanford. Stanford and Elgar sit as far apart as possible. (Radio Times Hulton Picture Lib.)

March the Elgars took a short lease on a flat in New Cavendish Street. It was there, after a chance meeting in the street, that Willie Reed was summoned to help settle the technical intricacies. It is interesting that Elgar felt a second opinion necessary, as he was a perfectly capable violinist himself. Reed 'found E. striding about with a lot of loose sheets of music paper, arranging them in different parts of the room. Some were already pinned on the backs of chairs, or stuck up on the mantelpiece ready for me to play . . . He had got the main ideas written out and, as he put it, "japed them up", to make a coherent piece.'

Kreisler had been trying to persuade Elgar to write a violin concerto for him for several years and it was to the great player that the work is dedicated. But there is a 'sub-dedication', a quote from Lesage's 'Gil Blas'; 'Aquí está encerra el alma de . . . . .' (Here is enshrined the soul of . . . . .). The five deliberate dots are another of Elgar's enigmas, and whether they stand for Alice (Stuart-Wortley or Elgar) or Julia (Worthington) is a matter of detective work and inclination. Whoever the true dedicatee, it was an acutely personal tribute, as he made clear in letters that June to Schuster and Alice Stuart-Wortley.

. . . it's *good!* awfully emotional! too emotional but I love it . . . : I have made the end serious & grand I hope . . . the music sings of memories and hope: This concerto is *full* of romantic feeling . . . I *know* the feeling is human and right – vainglory!

Hans Richter
(1843-1916).

Elgar duly conducted the first performance with Kreisler as soloist, as he had promised, on 10th November in the Queen's Hall at a concert promoted by the Philharmonic Society. There had been considerable competition between Richter, Henry Wood and the Philharmonic as to who should play it first for, coming eleven months after the Symphony, it was almost guaranteed to be a success. Elgar had, however, promised it to the Society and there was no going back on his word. He wrote to Richter

I have feared that you may have felt a little annoyed over the first performance of the Concerto being given here, but things were not quite in my own hands . . . My dear friend, you have from me all the love and reverence one man can feel for another. I feel a very small person when I am in your company, you who are so great and have been intimate with the greatest. I meet now many men, and I want you to know that I look to you as my greatest and most genuine friend in the world.

Well he might, for if it had not been for Richter's championship of the *Variations* Elgar's fame would surely have been slower to grow. Richter never conducted the concerto for, although only sixty-seven, his sight was failing and within a few months he resigned from the Hallé Orchestra, retired from conducting and returned to the Continent, where he died in 1916.

The Concerto was as successful as had been expected and Kreisler played it throughout the land, mainly conducted by Henry Wood. Across the channel Ysaÿe took it up. In one memorable performance in Brussels the following March he played it under Elgar's conductorship and then sat amongst the first violins as a member of the orchestra for the First Symphony. Sadly and inexplicably, although both Kreisler and Ysaÿe lived well into the age of electric recording, neither ever committed their thoughts to wax, leaving that honour to the young Yehudi Menuhin in 1932.

After the Violin Concerto had been completed, and while it was waiting for its November introduction, Elgar continued to work on the Second Symphony, the themes for which had begun to emerge in Italy at the same time. He was writing faster and to greater purpose than ever before, and on 29th January he told Alice Stuart-Wortley, 'I have recorded last year in the first movement, to which I put the last note in the score a moment ago and I must tell you this: I have worked at fever heat and the thing is tremendous in energy.' The second movement is a lament, for King Edward, whom Elgar had liked as a person as well as a monarch, but also for Alfred Rodewald, whose death in 1903 had so upset him. The whole work was completed on the last day of February and Alice Elgar could write in her diary, 'it seems one of his very greatest works, vast in design, and supremely beautiful . . . it résumés our human life, delight, regrets, farewell, the saddest mood & then the strong man's triumph.' a description that could as aptly apply to Mahler's Ninth (also worked on in 1909-10) as Elgar's Second Symphony. Neither were to finish another.

Between the Second Symphony's completion and its performance in May 1911 Elgar went with the Sheffield Choir on their tour of Canada and the United States. He did not enjoy himself. Professor Sanford, his friend at Yale, was dead and so the main pleasure he found in that country had been removed. He found it 'so raw and silly out here', and that 'every nerve is shattered by some angularity, vulgarity, and general horror'. He never found it necessary to cross the Atlantic again. While abroad, he worked on purely English themes. George V was to be crowned that summer and for the event Elgar was asked for a new march and an 'offertorium' for the service.

Queen's Hall was not full for the 2nd Symphony, as it had been for the first, partly because the price of tickets was high and partly because concerts that consist of three contemporary works (the other composers represented on this occasion were Bantock and Walford Davies) do not often draw large audiences. Elgar, however, was not the man to see such realities in these pragmatic terms. He conducted the first performance on 24th May, six days after Mahler's death in Vienna. The mourning in Austria and the mood of the elegiac work did not reflect London's spirit in the summer of a Coronation when Britain was, and felt, at the height of its power. There was no standing on the seats this time. The press spoke of 'cordial warmth' and 'much enthusiasm'. To Elgar, though, the audience seemed 'like a lot of stuffed pigs' and it was a failure; so it remained until the young Adrian Boult took up the

Elgar with some of the Sheffield Choir on a station platform in the American Mid-West, 1911. He did not enjoy the trip.

cause after World War I when its restless nostalgia was far more in tune with the times. Although both symphonies are basically optimistic, the similarity ends there. Whereas the First is magnificent and overpowering, *'nobilmente'* at its grandest, the Second is contemplative and searching. Rather than appealing to the listener immediately it grows in stature with repeated hearings. Perhaps if more of the first night audience had attended the second performance a fortnight later, the equality between the two symphonies might have been recognised earlier. Even now, it is not as popular as the A flat Symphony: the conflict between Elgar's public music and his private music is never far below the surface. For his public face, audiences had only to wait until the Coronation: for another deeply felt private work they had to wait until well after the War, by which time memories of that glorious, confident and Imperial summer had completely faded.

By 1912 Elgar had largely achieved all he had set out to do. He was the country's greatest living composer; he had, with *Gerontius*, *The Introduction and Allegro*, the First Symphony, and the *Enigma Variations*, revolutionised both the regard of his countrymen for native music and the stature of England as a musical nation abroad. He was knighted, bemedalled, applauded: the great peaks of his career had been climbed: he had become, at the age of fifty-five, a national institution.

The coming years were ones of restlessness and an awareness of the fragility of all he had built. Few compositions that did not have their roots in old ideas were written, except for pot-boilers or wartime commissions. In music there were new and, to Elgar, strange, forces at work that were making his style out of date. While he had despised the impotence of nineteenth century English music, he had essentially worked within its limitations and romantic principles. He did not really approve of Debussy: how then was he to cope with the barbaric vigour of Stravinsky's *Rite of Spring* or the concepts of Schönberg? In spite of his fame and the apparent security of his reputation, he was still a lonely figure, as apart from the younger forces in music (with which he had always before identified) as he was from the academic establishment with whom he was never entirely comfortable.

Alice Elgar, however, viewed the situation differently. Now that the genius she had married and encouraged was properly recognised, it was right that he should once again establish himself in London – not, this time, in an attempt to gain a foothold as they had tried so disastrously to do in the 1890s, but in triumph, taking their rightful place as members of the gentry. So Plas Gwyn was relinquished and for the last time Alice moved away from the counties of the Three Choirs. At Hampstead they found a house called Kelston which they re-named Severn House. It was large,

In the Garden of Severn House, Hampstead with Anthony Goetz, the young son of Muriel Foster, the contralto who sang in many of Elgar's works.

Lady Elgar at the window
of Severn House, c. 1912.

spacious and gloomy; designed in mock-Jacobean style by Norman Shaw. Troyte Griffith helped by designing the library and other friends, realising that despite Alice's ambitions Elgar was still not a wealthy man, helped out with the furnishings. There was a fine music-room, a picture gallery and, to Edward's delight, a billiard-room. But it was definitely beyond their means. Alice, however, was determined that nothing but a prosperous and respectable front should be presented to the outside world even if it meant a budgetary struggle. She was not young and eventually the strain told. But all this was realised only by the family and the close circle of friends that protectively surrounded them.

One thing that made the move to London a necessity rather than a luxury was Elgar's acceptance of the Principal Conductorship of the London Symphony Orchestra for the 1911/12 season, in succession to Richter. As well as planning programmes and a series of London concerts, he toured with the orchestra and conducted at the major provincial festivals. This was work he enjoyed, for he felt more at home with orchestral players than any other body of people. He felt one of them (as, indeed, he had been not very long before) and conducting gave him a less emotionally exhausting outlet for his musical energy. Normally such a post would have brought him a comfortable fee, but the orchestra's funds were low, and so rather than refuse or risk their solvency, he conducted them for nothing. Yet the money to run Severn House had to come from somewhere and symphonies, he knew by now, were not the answer. One solution was *The Crown of India*, an 'Imperial masque' mounted to celebrate the coronation of George V as Emperor of India. It was a rush job, thrown together in a month from odds and ends in his sketch books, but the opening night, on March 11th 1912, was a great success. The production was put on at the London Coliseum, now the home of English National Opera, but then a music-hall, albeit on a more imposing scale than most. Elgar conducted the whole run, and, if not particularly satisfying artistically, it had its rewards.

When I write a big serious work e.g. Gerontius, we have had to starve and go without fires for twelve months as a reward: this small effort allows me to buy scientific works I have yearned for . . .

When the masque closed he was ordered to rest, for his old ear complaint had returned and he suffered from twinges of gout. During the spring he visited Schuster at Bray, the Speyers at Ridgehurst and friends in the Cotswolds. As had happened in previous years, the change of routine stimulated him to work. He had been thinking of a setting for Arthur O'Shaughnessy's poem *The Music Makers* for about nine years and the time seemed right for the completion of the project, to be ready for the Birmingham Festival in the Autumn.

The Music Makers is the last of Elgar's great choral works and occupies a pivotal position in his output. It has never enjoyed the popularity of the oratorios and the criticisms levelled against it (that it is self-indulgent, overblown and that the poem is dated, sentimental and inadequate) are not without some foundation. However, no matter what the audience's reaction, for Elgar it was desperately important: the summary of his views on the role of the artist and the obstacles it was his duty to overcome. In this, as in the Violin Concerto and the Second Symphony, he 'bared his soul'. Indeed, he regarded the three works as a loose trilogy: they share an elegiac quality – a nostalgia – that was to grow even more evident in *Falstaff*, the late chamber music and the Cello Concerto.

As well as the wider aspects of the artist's role that are discussed by the poem, Elgar makes it clear in the music, by the use of extensive quotation from his earlier works, that it is as much a self-portrait as Strauss's *Ein Heldenleben* (A Hero's Life). In fact a comparison with Strauss's work throws interesting light on Elgar's. Whereas Strauss is boisterous and self-confident, Elgar is nervous and nostalgic. Where the quotations in *Ein Heldenleben* are aired as an act of defiance, those in *The Music Makers* illustrate his apartness from other men. The most noticeable reference is to the *Enigma* theme, which he always regarded as an expression of loneliness, a world within himself that was not only the source of the composer's inspiration but also of his unhappiness, that Elgar was coming to realise, could not be dispelled merely by material recognition. To this dilemma *The Music Makers* poses two solutions: firstly, the understanding of his friends. This work is dedicated to Nicholas Kilburn, the faithful amateur conductor who had always championed him, but in the music there are references, via earlier dedications, to others; Jaeger (a marvellous setting for contralto of Nimrod), Schuster and Alice Stuart-Wortley. Secondly there was the solace of retreat into the world of his imagination, as the opening verse of the text implies:-

> We are the music makers,
> And we are the dreamers of dreams,
> Wandering by lone sea-breakers,
> And sitting by desolate streams . . .

Elgar was obsessed with dreams; they recur throughout his works, and with increasing frequency, often linked with a feeling of wistful remembrance (as in the *Wand of Youth* Suites; *Dream Children* and the 'Peter Pan' world of *The Starlight Express; The Sanguine Fan*, the very late *Nursery Suite* and in *Falstaff*, with the hero asleep and full of wine) or with a vision, as in this work and, most obvious of all, *The Dream of Gerontius*.

Stylistically, there is no doubt that *The Music Makers* was a very backward-looking work for 1912; a choral cantata more at home with Parry's treatment of a similar subject, *Blest Pair of Sirens* (1887). And perhaps Elgar felt this, for at the time he orchestrated the work (during July), he was doing the same service to a song he had written twenty years before, *The Wind at Dawn*.

Although they had only moved to London eight months earlier, the Elgars had no intentions of giving up their connections with the West Country completely and so, for the summer, they took a house in Hereford for the Three Choirs Festival. The songs he had been orchestrating were performed, but for once there was no major new work as *The Music Makers* was reserved for Birmingham's Festival immediately afterwards. In the event, it was to be the last, but one of the greatest, of the triennial gatherings there, and it is appropriate that the city which had commissioned the oratorios should have had the last of his choral works as its own swan song.

Elgar found London no more congenial a place in which to work or to relax than when he had first settled there, despite the fact that ease of access meant that he was properly part of the international musical and artistic set for the first time. Among those who visited him during these years were Siegfried Wagner, Siloti, Chaliapin, Paderewski and Henry James. Even though he had settled near Hampstead Heath – almost a stretch of country within London – he was pining for Worcestershire, and felt again the loneliness that can only be suffered in big cities. The day after he finished *The Music Makers* he wrote to Alice Stuart-Wortley:-

Yesterday was the most *awful* day which inevitably occurs when I have completed a work: it has always been so: but this time I promised myself *a day*! . . . But . . . Alice and Carice were away for the day & I wandered alone on the Heath – it was bitterly cold – I wrapped myself in a thick overcoat & sat for two minutes, tears streaming out of my cold eyes and loathed the world, came back to the house – empty and cold – how I hated having written anything . . .'

However unhelpful he found the capital, he had to return there in the Autumn and get back to work once the first performance of *The Music Makers* was safely out of the way. He had accepted a commission for a symphonic work from Leeds to be given at the 1913 Festival – all the acrimony of ten years before had been forgotten, it seems – but, as on that occasion, he could not settle down to composing. Once again he tried the expedient of a month in Italy that had worked so successfully when he had been stuck before. January in Naples stimulated the right idea, one which he had thought of originally several years earlier: a tone poem in the manner of Strauss's *Don Quixote* depicting the adventures of Shakespeare's Falstaff. The sketches were duly revived but detailed work still eluded him when he returned to London. Neither a solitary trip to the Welsh spa of Llandrindod Wells nor a visit to his sister at Stoke proved to be the answer. His listlessness was deepened further by the news that Lord Northampton, a close friend whom he had met through Schuster, had died, and within days so had Julia Worthington (in New York; of cancer).

Once away from the stultifying atmosphere of London and given the freedom of the summer house at The Hut, however, the score progressed. Most of June and July were spent there, while Alice

Three Choirs Festival, Gloucester 1913. Two organists, Lloyd and Brewer, stand with Elgar behind the French composer Camille Saint-Saëns. (Radio Times Hulton Picture Lib.)

remained at Hampstead. Elgar worked amid the encouragement and admiration of friends like Frances Colvin, the painter Percy Anderson and the splendidly-titled Ranee of Sarawak. A garden by the river was a perfect place to be illustrating the escapades of Falstaff, Prince Hal and Pistol. Very little time at all was spent at Severn House in the middle months of 1913: a family holiday in the Welsh town of Penmaenmawr and the usual round of festivals saw to that. At Gloucester, where, as well as *Gerontius* (becoming almost inevitable at a Three Choirs meeting), the Second Symphony was also played, Elgar met Saint-Saëns.

The Leeds Festival at the end of September had engaged Elgar as conductor as well as the provider of *Falstaff*, and he was required to conduct a series of concerts whose length would be regarded as intolerable now and could not have seemed much better then. In one *Gerontius*, Brahms's Third Symphony and *Alto Rhapsody* were further augmented by works by Parry and Beethoven, an event that must have lasted for at least four hours even without intervals. It was in such a programme that *Falstaff* received its first performance; small wonder that the reception was less than ecstatic. Although Elgar regarded it as amongst his finest works it is not easy to bring off, for (despite his remarks on the subject in his Birmingham lecture of seven years earlier) it has a detailed and exact literary programme. Consequently, unless the conductor is able to give it an all-embracing shape, it can sound disjointed and rambling. In early performances it suffered, for Elgar was perhaps too engrossed in the cleverness of his Shakespearean allusions and the wealth of orchestral description. Whatever its faults, *Falstaff* does show a deep knowledge of the subject, which had its roots in the childhood stories told by Ned Spiers and the hours of browsing above the Worcester music shop. Landon Ronald, to whom the work was dedicated, admitted that he could not 'make head or tail of it'. *Falstaff* had to wait for the championship of interpreters like Boult and Barbirolli before the composer's high opinion could be shared by audiences.

Elgar's *Falstaff*, unlike Shakespeare's portrayal in the first part of *Henry IV* or *The Merry Wives of Windsor*, is rarely a bawdy drunken buffoon. He never seems genuinely wicked. Instead he is a genial old man, rambling, given to sentimental memories and to nodding off, but with a mischievous and engaging sense of fun. He is bewildered and hurt by his banishment and he dies lonely and misunderstood. The portrait is uncomfortably close to Elgar's self-pitying vision of himself. Nevertheless, in spite of the disinterested reaction in Leeds, the tone-poem was performed in Manchester and London (to a 'beggarly row of half-empty benches') before the end of the year.

Madresfield Court, Tudor seat of the Lygon family, Earl Beauchamp, in the Severn Valley.

From the north Elgar returned to Worcestershire, happy to visit Caractacus's camp and to stroll along the Malvern hills. He stayed with Earl Beauchamp at Madresfield Court, the beautiful ancestral home of the Lygon family since the fifteenth century in the country between Malvern and the Severn. Elgar had been associated with the Lygons for many years, or at least with Lady Mary's amateur music festivals at Madresfield. Nevertheless, it was a measure of how far up the social ladder he had climbed that he was now accepted as a fêted guest at a stately home near the same town where, only twenty-four years before, his wife's middle-class acquaintances had declined to meet a mere violin teacher, the son of a local tradesman. Nowadays these distinctions seem anachronistic and largely irrelevant, but then they were the forces without which society could not be considered to function.

Change was in the air: Elgar had noted the new undercurrents as early as 1910 in a letter to Schuster. The war that was to break within a year of his visit to Madresfield Court was finally to reduce much that remained of the Victorian way of life to absurdity. Some of the old ways and old attitudes survived the war but, like Elgar himself, the fire had gone out of them.

6   War and Twilight Works

Perhaps by way of compensation for the coming turmoil, the weather behaved impeccably in 1914. The winter was mild and Elgar was comfortably ensconced at Severn House tinkering with old ideas. Nothing on a large scale was planned, though representatives came to try and persuade him to think again about the third part of his oratorio trilogy. He seemed to agree but took it no further. However, one small piece, *Carissima*, did herald new, and increasingly important, activity. On January 21st Elgar went to a recording studio for the first time to put the new work on wax, even before its première.

Landon Ronald, who had been Musical Adviser to the Gramophone Company since 1900 and who was to conduct *Carissima* on 15th February had achieved a considerable coup in getting Elgar to the studio, for until then no composer of any reputation had taken the gramophone as a medium for orchestral music seriously. For a start there was the objection that only four minutes of music could be fitted onto each side of a disc. Then there was the acoustic system of recording by which the artists sat around a horn extending into the studio, which channelled the sound directly to a needle cutting in a continuous spiral towards the centre of a wax disc. Only a few instruments could be clustered close enough to the horn to give satisfactory definition to the sound, and so pieces had to be recorded with a severely reduced band of players. Some instruments recorded better than others. For example, while violins could be recorded with reasonable fidelity, the piano sounded like a muffled tin can and the French horn emerged as a muddy blur.

None of this mattered very much to Elgar, however. The offer came at precisely the right moment, for he felt in a creative rut – there were no fresh ideas in the offing – and his conducting pride had taken a damaging knock when the London Symphony Orchestra had declined to extend his principal conductorship

Landon Ronald and Fritz Kreisler outside the headquarters of the Gramophone Company at Hayes, Middlesex. (EMI).

beyond 1913. Also, the same enthusiasm for all things scientific, that had led him to build his laboratory at Plas Gwyn, made it inevitable that the new technology of the gramophone should intrigue him, especially when it gave him the opportunity of setting down his personal interpretation of his own music within weeks of its composition or first performance. Normally he reacted angrily to any attempt to meddle with his orchestration (Sir Adrian Boult once told me that Elgar was very sharp with him when he tried to reduce the orchestra for a touring performance of *Gerontius* in the early 1920s), but the challenge offered by recording overcame all his misgivings.

The recording of *Carissima* took place in the 'His Master's Voice' studios at 21 City Road in the East End of London, on an upper floor to escape from the noise and vibration of traffic. The recording was successful (by no means a foregone conclusion in those days) and the final pressing was in the shops by the beginning of April. One fringe benefit to be gained from Elgar's new relationship with The Gramophone Company was the installation of their latest machine at Severn House which not only provided hours of entertainment, but also a marvellous excuse for laziness as Alice noted in her diary in March:- 'E. much inclined to play with anything to avoid working at Anthem.' But he was not satisfied with anything less than the best: one machine was sent back because it did not have full enough tone, and on another occasion a man was sent round to see the colour of the study panelling so that a better matching cabinet could be provided.

Besides *Carissima* he composed a few part-songs (Op. 71-73) and an anthem for St. Paul's Cathedral, but more time was taken up with re-arranging works for recording. By the end of June he had signed a contract with The Gramophone Company, by which he was paid £50 and a 5 per cent royalty, and committed to wax two of the *Bavarian Dances*, *Salut d'amour*, and *Pomp and Circumstance Marches* Nos. 1 and 4. This time the studio was at the new company headquarters at Hayes in West Middlesex, now a nondescript industrial suburb of London, but then very different. Alice in her diary entry for the 26th June described the visit:-

Lovely day. A. drove on & stopped by a nice hayfield & then on to Hayes Church, sweet old place & village – beautiful trees & birds pouring out song in the churchyard. A. asked in & heard some of the playing & given tea. Then lovely drive back.

His recording engagements disposed of, Elgar and his family left to spend July in Scotland at the village of Gairloch in Ross, where he could gaze across the Minches to the northern tip of Skye and, in the distance, to the Isle of Lewis. The quiet was perfect and while he took Carice fishing on the loch for hours, Alice spent her time writing or watching the sheep basking on the sand at the water's edge. It was while they were there that, on August 4th, the war which had threatened for years became a reality. As they travelled back to England they saw the troops marching out from Inverness and Edinburgh.

In London they found an air of forced normality. On August 15th the Proms opened as usual. When Henry Wood had suggested cancelling them Robert Newman, manager of the Queen's Hall Orchestra, snapped:- 'Not *run* them?! Why not? The war can't last three months and the public will need its music and, incidentally, our orchestra its salaries.' It was an optimistic view shared by many. England, after all, had not been involved in a

The first of Elgar's recording sessions – at the old City Road studio – 1914. (EMI).

major European war since the defeat of Napoleon a century before. To Alice it was all wonderfully stirring, and to that Promenade audience *Land of Hope and Glory* took on a greater significance than ever. In the same programme was a new Elgar work, *Sospiri*, a quiet, sad piece for string orchestra that fitted ill with the mood of the nation but, contrasted with his imperial hymn, well illustrated Elgar's own private misgivings.

On the one hand he was a fervent patriot and keenly aware of a sense of national duty. This was the side of his nature which he made public throughout the war years, always ready with occasional pieces for fund-raising or exhortation. On the other hand, he was fully aware of the horror of war and found nothing in it to glorify. Above all, he hated the cruelty to the innocent; he wrote to Schuster:

Concerning the war I say nothing – the only thing that wrings my heart and soul is the thought of the horses – oh! my beloved animals – the men and women can go to hell – but my horses . . .

He had other reasons for regretting war. In the same letter he said:-

94

Everything is at a standstill & we have nothing left in the world – absolute financial ruin . . .

The war did not stop music making altogether, but severely curtailed it (one of the first effects was the cancellation of the Worcester Festival) and for musicians who depended on piecemeal fees and royalties, whether composers or orchestral players, hardship was inevitable. More important, and more far-reaching, was the effect on his international reputation. All English music, never strong at the best of times, was under a complete moratorium. Richter, though privately less impassioned, was busily renouncing his English degrees; the hopes of Steinbach to perform *The Music Makers* in Düsseldorf now looked sadly ironic. With Vienna, Berlin and the Rhineland closed, Brussels occupied and St. Petersburg with plenty of other things to think about, the Continent was barred, particularly as the French had never been interested in Elgar anyway. Without the promptings of European musical fashion, America gradually lost interest as well. By the time the war ended new styles had come to maturity and Elgar seemed a survivor from a past age. His position abroad has never recovered.

There was, of course, a corresponding attempt to exclude German music from British concerts, but this met with more opposition. Ernest Newman, writing in the *Musical Times* a month after the outbreak of war, put the case against bigotry clearly:

Musicians may well doubt the sanity of a world in which Kreisler is in arms against Ysaÿe and Thibaud, in which it is the business of those of us here who owe some of the finest moments of our life to the great living German composers to do all we can to prevent their pouring out any more of their genius upon us.

This same line was taken by Robert Newman and Henry Wood, who were under great pressure to emasculate the Prom prospectus:

They [the Directors of the Queen's Hall Orchestra] take this opportunity of emphatically contradicting the statements that German music will be boycotted during the present season. The greatest examples of Music and Art are world possessions and unassailable even by the prejudices and passions of the hour.

For the first two years of the war, however, each Prom concert began with three Allied national anthems, to the intense boredom of Henry Wood who had to conduct them. Xenophobia must have its sacrificial victims, and in a spectacular display of public idiocy,

Elgar's friends Sir Edgar and Lady Speyer (who were German by birth) were driven to emigrate to America by the taunts and threats of the press, even though they had contributed over £30,000 to English music and been the main backers of the Promenade Seasons for years.

However depressed he may have been by the repercussions of war, Elgar was no pacifist and he joined the Special Constabulary (Constable 0015014, S. Division) as a Staff Inspector immediately on his return from Scotland, transferring to the Hampstead Volunteer Reserve the following year. Alice was active on endless charitable committees and at one point taught French to the troops. But of course the greatest contribution was musical. Severn House's music room was used for small fund-raising concerts, while Elgar himself conducted at larger events.

His first opportunity to compose occasional music came with the occupation of Belgium in the autumn. The reported German atrocities evoked a wave of sympathy in England and Elgar caught the mood perfectly by providing an orchestral backing for a recitation of *Carillon*, a short poem by the Belgian writer Emile Cammaerts. It was first performed on December 7th with the poet's wife reciting in French. Elgar included it in every programme during a tour with the London Symphony Orchestra that he conducted immediately afterwards. He recorded an English version with Henry Ainley as the speaker at the end of January 1915, and conducted the work in London again the following month, before the records went on sale.

In the Spring he tried to emulate the success of *Carillon* by repeating the formula in *Une Voix dans le Désert* and later with *Le Drapeau Belge*, again by Cammaerts, but these were not as popular as his first attempt. Between the Belgian pieces came a short symphonic prelude, *Polonia*, composed as the centre-piece of a

The Hampstead Special Constabulary 1914. Constable 0015014, S Division, Staff Inspector Elgar stands at the bottom left of the picture.

concert in aid of the Polish Relief Fund. This piece includes the Polish national anthem, a Chopin Nocturne and a folk-song arranged by Paderewski. These works were not professional opportunism on Elgar's part, for all the proceeds went to the various wartime funds for which they were written.

The alternative to facing the horrors of the war was to escape from them and so when the actress and producer Lena Ashwell asked Elgar for a few songs to go into a children's play for the Kingsway Theatre, he accepted with relish. The play was *The Starlight Express* by Algernon Blackwood and was similar in feeling both to Barrie's 'Peter Pan' and to the imaginary world the Elgar children had created nearly fifty years earlier: a world he had already enshrined in the *Wand of Youth*. Adults messed things up and only children had the necessary vision – poignantly true, given the ineptitude of Allied Command.

The project was irresistible for Elgar, allowing him to give free rein to his pre-occupation with dreams and childhood, and his involvement grew. Eventually there were orchestral dances as well as twelve songs and incidental music to back the dialogue. He had, perhaps unwittingly, written a semi-opera in the tradition of the late seventeenth century. An audience familiar with the world of Locke and Shadwell's 'The Tempest' or Purcell's 'Faery Queen' would have found nothing strange in *The Starlight Express*. Dryden's definition of opera – 'a poetical tale or fiction, represented by vocal and instrumental musick, adorned with scenes, machines and dancing' – fits it well. It was certainly the nearest Elgar ever got to completing a full-length work for the operatic stage. The production itself was not a success and only ran for a month (January 1916). One reason was the scenery, which Elgar disliked so much that he refused to conduct and did not even attend the first night (an unprecedented step for him though he and Alice did go to the last performance); another was the unsatisfactory adaptation by Violet Pearn of Blackwood's original text. Neither was Blackwood happy with the show, but he and Elgar became firm friends and he attended the recording sessions which took place at Hayes in February with Agnes Nicholls and Charles Mott as the soloists.

At the same time Elgar's contract with The Gramophone Company was renewed, by which he now received a flat payment of £100 per annum and an extra £21 for every session (four were guaranteed each year).

Almost a year before he had been given a book of poems, originally published in 'The Times', called 'The Winnowing Fan' by his friend Laurence Binyon who worked (as did Sidney Colvin) at the British Museum. He started to set three of them, 'To Women', 'The Fourth of August' and 'For the Fallen', but when

A poster for the Starlight Express, Christmas 1915.

he found that another composer, Cyril Rootham, had already agreed to set 'For the Fallen' for Novello's he abandoned the project. Nevertheless his friends, led by Binyon, urged him to continue, which he did, but only after Rootham's setting had been published – a generous gesture to a younger composer, not that Rootham recognised it as such.

Elgar finished *For the Fallen* early in March and it received its first performance in Leeds on May 4th 1916. Three days later it came to the Queen's Hall where, with *Gerontius*, it was performed in aid of the Red Cross every night for a week, attended by several members of the Royal family. Binyon's poem contains one of the most famous of all Great War verses, still recited on Remembrance Sunday each year – 'At the going down of the sun and in the morning . . . We will remember them' – and Elgar's setting remains one of the most sensitive elegies for the dead. The other two movements were not finished until the following year, when the whole work was given the title *The Spirit of England*; however, 'For the Fallen' is more often performed separately.

Between the completion and first performance of *For the Fallen* Elgar had been taken ill on a train and, after several days in a nursing home, was ordered to rest. He was suffering from a disease of the ear which had often troubled him, but it was now compounded by exhaustion and depression brought on partly by the strain of living in London in wartime and partly by the continual worry about money, which, with the expense of running a large town house, travelling round the country to conduct, and receiving nothing for his many charity engagements, was becoming an increasing problem. The strain took its toll on Alice too, for she was nearing seventy and was still as active, if not more so, than she had been throughout the twenty-seven years of their marriage.

Elgar was unwell for the rest of 1916 and became more and more convinced that he could never be happy or work properly in a town. By January 1917 he was refusing to see visitors, but this desperate low point (which had always heralded a new surge of creativity) was soon over. It was a set of records of his violin concerto which did the trick this time. The recording sessions had taken place the previous month and the soloist was Marie Hall, who had been recording since 1904, but more importantly, she was the one great success of Elgar's days spent teaching the violin in Malvern. It was not, in fact, the work's first appearance on disc, as Henry Wood and Albert Sammon's account for the rival Columbia label had been issued earlier that year. The day fixed for the recording was dominated by the weather ('Frightful fog . . . Very horrid', Alice wrote). During the drive to Hayes a cart ran into their car: on the return journey they narrowly missed a further accident when a Red Cross van loomed up on the wrong side of the

Marie Hall (1884-1956), Elgar's one successful violin pupil. He recorded the violin concerto with her in 1916.

road. Despite these mishaps the actual sessions were a great success. When he heard the finished results Elgar was delighted and, not surprisingly, concluded that his version was far superior to Wood's.

In February he was still unwell and confined to bed with a heavy cold. But his depression lifted somewhat when a Mrs. Ina Lowther called to ask him to write a ballet, *The Sanguine Fan*, for a matinée to be performed in Chelsea in aid of war charities. He accepted: mainly, perhaps, because the idea of asking him had originally come from Alice Stuart-Wortley. The scenario was an escapist eighteenth century tableaux based on a sanguine (red) fan, drawn by the artist Charles Conder, showing Pan and Echo disporting amongst gentlefolk in a sylvan glade. For this innocent panorama he provided music, lasting about a quarter of an hour, which has the charm of *Salut d'amour* but also something of the abandoned frenzy of Ravel's choreographic poem *La Valse*. It was Elgar's only ballet, but it is another example of his growing fascination with the stage since his move to London five years before. Since 1911 only

Fred Gaisberg, one of the two American brothers who were the driving force behind the classical side of HMV in its early days. (EMI).

The Music Makers, *The Spirit of England* and the two orchestral miniatures *Carissima* and *Sospiri* had been written for the concert hall.

He was now working at full throttle once more and *The Sanguine Fan* was hardly out of the way before he started on another orchestral song-cycle, once again using the sea as the unifying theme. This time he turned to Kipling for his text (rather more satisfactory verse than he had found for *Sea Pictures*) and such was his enthusiasm for the theatre that he approached the Coliseum (where *The Crown of India* had been put on) about the viability of including the cycle, to be called *The Fringes of the Fleet*, in the programme, with Charles Mott as the lead singer and a small chorus.

While these plans were going ahead (none too smoothly since they involved persuading the War Office to postpone Mott's call-up) Elgar was busy orchestrating *The Spirit of England* and abridging *Cockaigne* and the *Prelude and Angel's Farewell* from *Gerontius* for the gramophone. During the course of one day at the end of February he made a total of seven records, including the first of the *Bavarian Dances* and the *Tame* and *Wild Bears* movements from *The Wand of Youth*, as well as the pieces just mentioned. Gradually 'His Master's Voice' was building up as complete a catalogue of his music as was technically possible, and documenting each new work with the original artists as it appeared. Today this merely seems like good sense, but in 1916 the gramophone industry, like the cinema, was still in its infancy. It is a tribute to the far-sightedness of both Elgar and the Gaisberg brothers at H.M.V. that the far from adequate new medium should be taken seriously. No other composer had such an opportunity at so early a stage: the records he made at that time, though the music is often curtailed and mercilessly re-moulded, are still fascinating and, moreover, are still generally available.

The Fringes of the Fleet was worked on until the middle of May and final rehearsals got under way in the early part of June. Elgar was shown over the fleet at Harwich, through the good offices of Lady Warrender, to push him into the spirit of the occasion and the performances opened on June 11th. It was the only really jingoistic music Elgar wrote during the war: all the rest either showed the misery of conflict or ignored the subject altogether. Coming as they did at a point when the Western Front seemed to be in a position of utter stalemate, the songs were just the sort of boost of confidence the nation needed. On the first night a suitably nautical audience was gathered including a clutch of Admirals, among them Lord Beresford, whose warnings on the unpreparedness of the Royal Navy Alice had found 'thrilling' in 1909. Elgar had planned that *Fringes* should initially run only for a month, but it was still drawing the crowds well into July. After touring to Manchester and Leicester it returned to the Coliseum for a final period, its popularity now reinforced by the release of the records made during July. For some unaccountable reason the otherwise unalloyed joy of the work's success was interrupted half way through its run by Kipling, who objected to Elgar's settings. Eventually, after some grumbling, he subsided and all continued as before.

As usual, the pattern of Elgar's temperament dictated that such a period of creative activity should be followed by a progressive decline until it reached a point as dismally low as that which had preceded it. Consequently, as the autumn progressed and the war continued, the euphoria of his latest triumph evaporated: his health worsened and the old pre-occupation with the countryside became paramount once again. In September he wrote, while conducting *Fringes of the Fleet* at Chatham, to Alice Stuart-Wortley:

I am not well and the place is so noisy & I do not sleep. The guns are the quietest things here. I long for the country . . . Everything good & nice & clean & fresh & sweet is far away – never to return.

By the end of 1917 his doctor was sufficiently worried by his general condition to insist that he be examined by a specialist. Nothing appeared to be physically wrong, although his health showed no signs of improvement. The family had realised for some time that he needed some sort of bolt-hole in the country, and so Alice and Carice duly went in search of one. The answer proved to be a thatched cottage near Fittleworth in West Sussex, which had a dilapidated but refurbishable studio in a large garden, woods and a fine view. It was as near a substitute for Birchwood as they were likely to find within easy distance of London. Proximity to the capital was important for family unity, if nothing else, for whatever Elgar's need for the country, his wife and daughter needed the society and entertainment of London just as much.

1918 began gloomily. After further inspection by doctors it was decided that his tonsils needed removing and he went into a nursing-home for the operation. Whatever the medical merits of this diagnosis, the relief that followed definite action seemed to clear his mind, and while still in hospital he started sketching new themes. To convalesce he went to stay first with Frank Schuster at Bray and then, in April, to the Sussex cottage, 'Brinkwells'. The result of finding himself once again in the country, in a house that was his for an indefinite period, was little short of miraculous: it was almost as though the energy that he had found twenty years before had fully returned. He started on four major works at the

Brinkwells, the cottage near Fittleworth in West Sussex, where Elgar re-found the peace of Birchwood and wrote the late Chamber music.

same time; three chamber works (an area he had started to explore on at least three previous occasions, but had always abandoned) and the Cello Concerto.

There are several possible reasons why Elgar should have suddenly turned to chamber music after a comparatively uneventful, or at least unprofound, period. There was a desire to return to abstract forms of expression. He had written nothing without a text or programme of any consequence since the second symphony seven years before, and whatever he may have written in between, there is no reason to suppose that his views on the artistic value of absolute music had changed since his Birmingham lectures. Behind his concern for the purity of composition there was, perhaps, a feeling (based on his admiration for the late quartets of Beethoven) that the exploration of chamber music should be the culmination of a composer's career. Just as it had taken him until he was fifty to find the resources to write a symphony, so it took him till his sixties to feel satisfied with his ability to cope with the concentrated demands of the sonata, quartet and quintet. He had tried to write a quartet that pleased him since 1878 (one he took as far as labelling Op.8 before destroying it) but only now, once more in the quiet of the woods and with a new clarity to his thoughts, was he able to come to terms with these forms. It is, I think, possible to say that during the composition of the three chamber works, Elgar was for the first time truly at peace with himself; it was often a dark and brooding peace but there is an element of composure and self-knowledge in these works (especially the slow movement of the quartet) that contrasts markedly with the searching examination of the second symphony. Fame was no longer the spur. The bombast and orchestral richness that had been necessary to acquire that fame could now be abandoned, as could

102

Elgar with W.H. Reed; faithful friend, biographer and violinist collaborator.

London itself, in favour of autumnal restraint and reflection in a peaceful, rural atmosphere. It was a mood that had also affected the sick Debussy during the war and that, in a similar way, pervades his cello sonata, sonata for violin, harp and flute, and the final violin sonata.

Elgar's violin sonata was his first work to be completed in 1918. One inspiration was the landscape: perhaps the nearness of the woods and hills drew his mind back to his earlier 'Romance' for violin and piano (Op.1, 1878). Another was W.H. Reed, who became an increasingly frequent visitor to Fittleworth. He was one of the few people made welcome, since Elgar had chosen to live in his country retreat partly to escape the interruptions that friends inevitably entailed. By the time Reed had made his first visit during that summer, the first movement of the sonata was finished and the second was well on its way. He was met at the local station by Mr. Aylwin, the farmer whose pony and trap provided a rudimentary taxi service for visitors unfamiliar with the winding Sussex lanes that lead to Brinkwells.

At the top of the hill, looming on the sky-line, was what at first sight I took to be a statue; but as we drew nearer I saw it was a tall woodman leaning a little forward upon an axe with a very long handle. The picture was perfect and the pose magnificent . . . Sir Edward could not wait another moment to introduce me to the very heart of these woods, and to tell me all about the woodcraft which he had been learning . . . Chemistry, physics, billiards and music were abandoned and forgotten: nothing remained but an ardent woodman-cooper.

One might add to the list kite-flying, bicycling and golf, for there was more than a touch of Mr. Toad (from Wind in the Willows) to the way in which Elgar indulged his enthusiasms. To Reed, Lady Elgar said, 'I am so glad you have come: it is lovely for him to have someone to play with.' Whichever hobby was current he adopted with passionate dedication. Only fishing remained constant throughout his life.

Music was certainly not abandoned however, and with Reed on hand to try through passages as soon as they were written, the Sonata was finished by September. It was dedicated to an old friend, Marie Joshua, who, to Elgar's sadness, died only four days after he had inked in her name. In tribute he inserted a return to the music of the slow movement just before the coda of the final movement.

The String Quartet was begun immediately together with work on the Quintet. Into these went the moods of the Sussex autumn: the rain and gales, but also the glorious sunsets of the Arun valley and the favourite pastime of bonfire-building and cutting switches to make barrel hoops. Trees had always been a source of inspiration and near at hand were the sinister knarled trunks in Flexham Park, in legend the remains of Spanish monks struck by lightning and ossified while dabbling in black magic. To Alice they were depicted in the 'wonderful weird beginning' of the Quintet. Reed felt them (they gave him 'the creeps') in the 'mystical and fantastic theme of the second movement of the Sonata'. In the slow movement of the Quartet, too, there is a sudden moment of shadow in an otherwise lyrical calm, similar to those in the 13th variation in *Enigma* and the last movement of the Second Symphony.

In October, England's other 'countryman' composer, Sir Hubert Parry, died and Elgar interrupted his work to go to his funeral at St. Paul's Cathedral. Although the two were never intimate friends, there was a great deal of mutual respect and Elgar considered Parry the one composer of real worth to come from the academic establishment. At the same time the opportunity was taken to perform the new Sonata for half-a-dozen friends at Severn House, among them Muriel Foster and Landon Ronald. There were other engagements, but Elgar was only too eager to return to Sussex and to his music, for he now had a coherent idea of the cello concerto forming and he wanted to move the chamber works along as fast as he could.

He left London on the day the war ended, but he had long lost interest in it, feelings he expressed in a letter to Lawrence Binyon refusing to set his poem about peace:

I do not feel drawn to write peace music somehow . . . the whole atmosphere is too full of complexities for me to feel music to it; not the atmosphere of the poem but of the time I mean . . . the individual sorrow & sacrifice – a cruelty I resent bitterly & disappointedly.

Very different sentiments from those one might expect from the jingoistic Edwardian colonel of his public image! Lady Elgar, however, was as much a part of her military background as she had ever been. In September she had written in her diary of the 'real wood sounds & other lament wh. sh. be in a war symphony', a comment that shows not only her views on the time, but also how little she understood her husband's new mood.

It was becoming obvious that Severn House was now an unjustifiable drain on their finances, especially as Elgar insisted on maintaining Brinkwells. To Lady Elgar, who was depressed after a minor operation on her forehead, it was a bitter pill to swallow for London, where she could entertain, visit the aristocratic and famous and show off her 'genius' to society, was her life. To retreat again in the face of financial difficulties was too much like the failure of 1891. Her husband was not blind to the problem:

Sir Hubert Parry, Gloucestershire composer. The one composer in the English musical establishment for whom Elgar always maintained his respect.

the future is *dark* as A. poor dear is not well & of course is bored to death here while I am in the seventh heaven of delight . . . But it seems that if I have to live again at Hampstead composition is 'off' – not the house or the place but *London* – telephone etc. all day and night drives me mad.

Alice Elgar's distress in no way eased when, at the end of the year, Severn House was burgled. A whole range of possessions, from toast racks to socks, was taken, and it was small comfort nine months later when two former policemen were charged with the theft. To Lady Elgar this was further proof of the depths to which the country's moral standards had sunk.

On January 7th 1919 Reed was asked to organise a private performance of the Quartet and Piano Quintet, as he had done for the Sonata. Among the guests invited on this occasion was George Bernard Shaw, whom Elgar had met at a luncheon the year before and who was becoming less of an acquaintance and more of a friend. They were an unlikely pair, a staunch Irish Socialist and an English country Conservative. Politically it was a hopeless mismatch, especially since Elgar had signed the declaration pledging to fight Home Rule for Ireland in 1914. However Shaw had a deep regard for Elgar's music (in this he was a valuable ally) and, in his turn, Elgar had enough of the radical intellectual in him to enjoy Shaw's plays, even if he did not always agree with the conclusions. Lady Elgar thoroughly disapproved of them, but was prepared to forgive anybody who championed her husband's music.

The early part of 1919 was taken up with the domestic upheavals and reconstruction that inevitably followed the end of the war in November. Elgar had made no records during the previous year and so much of March, April and May were taken up with editing *Polonia*, *Chanson de nuit*, 'Nimrod' and 'Dorabella' from the *Variations*, and the rest of the *Wand of Youth* which had not been included in the previous set. In April Severn House was put on the market, but there appeared no immediate prospect of selling.

The Violin Sonata was given a semi-private performance on 13th March by W.H. Reed and Anthony Bernard for the British Music Society. The first public performance followed a week later at the Aeolian Hall, in New Bond Street, with Reed again playing the violin but with Landon Ronald as the pianist. The Quartet and Quintet had to wait until May, when they were given on 21st by a quartet consisting of Reed and Albert Sammons (violins), Raymond Jeremy (viola) and Felix Salmond (cello), with William Murdoch playing the piano part in the Quintet. The reception in the Wigmore Hall was warm, and Elgar went happily to Hayes the next day for the recording sessions of the four works mentioned above.

Salmond had been promised the first performance of the cello

The recording of The Sanguine Fan, 24th February 1920. Elgar conducts with Mrs. Cartaret Carey (wife of the governor of Windsor Castle), Princess Alice, Countess of Athlone, The Crown Prince of Rumania and the Earl of Athlone watching. It was the last session Lady Elgar attended before her death. (EMI).

concerto, and he soon followed the composer down to Brinkwells in the summer to iron out the details. Whatever Salmond's gifts as a musician, one person (as W.H. Reed recalled) who was completely nonplussed was Sir Edward's general Sussex factotum, Mark, who went with the cottage. Having considered the instrumentalist and his cello he 'silently withdrew'. 'That gentleman', Elgar informed him later, 'is a very famous musician, a great cellist, a very important person you know'. 'Well, I suppose it takes some of all sorts to make up a world' was the dour reply.

Summer at Brinkwells soon saw the concerto finished and the completed manuscript was ready to be posted to Novellos on August 8th. That the performance on October 26th 1919 was a disaster was the fault neither of Elgar nor of Salmond. Unlike the soloist in *Gerontius*, Salmond knew his part perfectly and Elgar's conducting was as sound as ever. The villain was Albert Coates who conducted the rest of the programme with the London Symphony Orchestra which consisted of Borodin's Second Symphony and Scriabin's *Poem of Ecstasy*, a work evidently needing a good deal more rehearsal time than was available. Unfortunately, Coates

Lady Elgar in old age.

Adrian Boult (b.1889), who conducted the first post-war performance of the Second Symphony on March 16th 1920.

decided to make time at Elgar's expense. He was kept waiting for an hour and as a result the concerto was hopelessly under-rehearsed at the concert. The critics put the blame firmly where it belonged, but a bad performance to an insignificant audience was not the launch Elgar had hoped for. The value of the new work, if not its première, was appreciated and H.M.V. were soon talking of recording it, not with Salmond (who was not under contract to them) but with the young Beatrice Harrison, another of Landon Ronald's protegés.

When Miss Harrison first came to Severn House to discuss and rehearse the concerto Lady Elgar had already been ill for a month. However, she seemed to rally with the start of the year and her doctors were not over-concerned. It had, after all, always been Sir Edward who had been ill and a worry before. But, to her friends, Alice was beginning to look far too frail. She was strong enough to go to the theatre and out to lunch, and to Hayes to watch the recording of some of *The Sanguine Fan* on 24th February, but she had to remain seated, much to her distress, during the entrance of royal visitors, the Crown Prince of Rumania and Princess Alice.

Although plainly fading, she still took delight in the new honours that came her husband's way. In February he was reconciled to the academic world finally when he was appointed to the Council of the Royal College of Music. On March 16th Adrian Boult, then thirty-one, conducted the first post-war performance of the Second Symphony at the Queen's Hall. The public was in a different mood from that of 1911 and now the richness of the music was seen for, as Boult said, 'they had been starved of that kind of contemporary music.' But also it was, as Muriel Foster rushed to tell him afterwards, a 'superb' reading. Lady Elgar was 'so thankful' for its success and was even more proud two days later when Elgar was made a member of the Académie des Beaux Arts in Paris.

Within a month, on 7th April 1920, she died of heart and kidney failure. Her life's work was accomplished for, although she had not achieved the literary fame she had once cherished, her adopted mission, to nurture a musical genius, had been fulfilled. Daughter of a baronet, she died the wife of a knight, a social distinction that meant a great deal to her, and one which her relations would never have believed possible on the day she married a poor Worcester violinist. Sir Adrian Boult's description is as accurate as any:

she was a small woman, rather timid and she spoke so quietly it was often difficult to hear her, but where Elgar was concerned, she was made of iron.

Three days later she was buried in the churchyard at Little Malvern, beneath the Herefordshire beacon. W.H. Reed brought his Quartet down and the slow movement of the String Quartet, which she had especially loved, was played.

An uninvited member of the congregation at the funeral service was Sir Charles Villiers Stanford who, desperately ill himself, felt that he must attend. In him, Elgar had a far stauncher friend than he was ever prepared to believe.

7 Ending in Worcestershire

With the death of his wife all Elgar's will to compose collapsed. He had always needed encouragement and reassurance in order to write anything of value, and nobody had believed in him with such faith or (sometimes suffocating) tenacity, as had Alice. What is more, that belief had always taken a practical form. She ruled his manuscript paper, posted his scores to publishers, answered letters when he was working and paid the bills. Her advice on each day's work was invaluable, not so much for its critical astuteness (though she was always ready to indicate anything she regarded as sub-standard), but for the sympathetic appreciation that prodded him on. She could be dull, prim, stuffy and humourless, and on these occasions he turned to his other close female friends for entertainment and relaxation. But, however fond he was of Dora Penny, Julia Worthington, Alice Stuart, Frances Colvin and the rest, in the end they were no substitute for his wife's devotion. He was never short of female admirers, for even in his sixties he was good-looking, but none of them were really prepared to sacrifice their entire way of life, as Alice had done, so that he could establish the steady monotonous routine needed for composition.

It was only with her death that he really realised just how poor he was (he and Carice were left with a fixed income of £200 per annum), and during that year there were enough reminders of his position to rake up some of his old radical fury against the monied classes. The first shock was the resurrection of the 'ancient hate and prejudice' of his wife's Victorian aunts, whose final act of class revenge had been to prevent the Roberts inheritance descending to any offspring of Elgar's. Then there was the news that two of his sisters were to be turned out of their houses by new owners, there being no satisfactory Rent Act at that time. He had spent some of his happiest days at Polly Grafton's farm at Stoke Prior and it was to there that he went immediately after the funeral. Alice had never visited Polly, so the house was free of those memories, and

Polly's husband had died a few years before, so he knew he could count on her understanding. The thought that she was to be evicted by the 'new rich' made him furious. In desperation he turned to a millionaire friend '& begged he would save it'. He told Alice Stuart,

he sympathised and sent an agent who reported it would only *pay four per cent* – so my friend could not entertain it!!! That is the end: the public have all my best work for nothing & I have not one single friend who cares . . . My whole past is wiped out & I am quite alone.

Indeed this seemed to be the case, for in the same week that the farm was advertised, Birchwood and all the banks of the Wye, where he had gone to fish and scribble down new themes, were sold. Brinkwells had also ceased to be a possible refuge, for the landlord changed his mind and refused to allow Elgar to stay on indefinitely.

He had never liked being in Hampstead and Severn House now seemed so desolate that he kept away for as much of the summer as he could. In September the Three Choirs Festival, dormant since 1913, was once again held at Worcester. Elgar rented the same rooms that his uncle Henry had lived in until his death three years before. It was a depressing festival, for so many of its former lights were dead, Parry and George Sinclair among them. Elgar was a sad and lonely figure, becoming an institution and, at the same time, a survivor from a vanished age.

Temperamentally he was not suited to the changed world of 1920. He was more adaptable than his wife had been, but so much had been swept away by the war. Some things he acknowledged were for the better, but he was frightened of the growth of socialism and the new values whether in society or music. He went to conduct in Amsterdam and Brussels (where King Albert invested him with the 'Ordre de la Couronne') but found that the Belgians had forgotten the war and seemed only to think of eating and drinking. At Christmas he went with his family to Stratford-on-Avon. Lunching at an hotel that was an old haunt, he found the management changed. 'U.S.A., I believe,' he wrote to Frances Colvin in disgust, 'A three weeks carnival at Christmas, *a Jazz band specially engaged* – dances every night – the whole place 'booked-up' with an abandoned set of filthy wretches! I have known S-on-A since 1869 and wish it cd. have been spared – we did not honour Shakespeare in this way in those sweet old years.' Others seemed better able to adjust to the change but Elgar could not. Frank Schuster visited him with 'some extraordinary females, friends of the youth whom F. introduces as his *nephew* – are we all mad!)'.

Beatrice Harrison
recording the cello
concerto with Elgar, 15th
November 1920. (EMI).

There was still, however, a protective circle to whom he could turn. Troyte Griffith alone remained an intimate from the *Enigma* days, and it was he who was asked to design a suitable headstone for Lady Elgar's grave and despatched to hunt for a new Malvern retreat. Alice Stuart (now Lady Stuart of Wortley) and Sir Sidney and Frances Colvin became closer than ever. Amongst the profession, W.H. Reed and Sir Ivor Atkins (the organist at Worcester) and Hugh Blair, his early patron but now less fortunate, remained staunch allies.

When he had to be in London, whether for meetings, conducting or recording, he spent his time at billiards, in one of the many clubs of which he was now a member (particularly favouring Brooks, the Saville and the Athenaeum), or at select dinner parties with his literary friends. At one such, in November 1920, he completed the fascinating quartet of Siegfried Sassoon, Sir James Barrie and Arnold Bennett, whose gathering it was.

Music seemed to be a forgotten occupation, discarded with the rest of his past. There was no further work on the piano concerto for Irene Scharrer, which he had been contemplating since 1909 and which he had hoped would follow the cello concerto. A trio for violin, cello and piano was similarly ignored. In the spring though, even if the creative spark was missing, the habits of a lifetime

The view across the Severn to the Malvern Hills from the garden of Napleton Grange. (photo: Jane Whitton).

broke through and he set about arranging Bach's C minor fugue for full orchestra. Strauss had said he would add the fantasia at the beginning, but since his contribution never materialised, Elgar set that as well in 1922. It shows Elgar at his most opulent, and if the inclusion of harps, trombones and cymbals does not appeal to those who like their Bach unadulterated, it does show the brilliance achieved by amalgamating the work of the greatest master of form with that of a master orchestrator. He performed the same service in 1923 for the Worcester Festival, setting the Overture to Handel's Second Chandos Anthem.

He finished the Bach fugue in May and began looking again at the sketches for the third part of *The Apostles*. But the interest was not sustained: a new period of unhappiness set in engendered by the realisation, long in coming, of the finality of his bereavement. He was to be even more alone, for Carice was soon to be married. Sadly, in August 1921, he left Brinkwells and moved out of Severn House in October. He now occupied a small flat 'just sitting room, bedroom, bathroom, etc. . . .', in St. James's Place, close to his clubs and not too far from Queen's Hall. He continued throughout this difficult period to take an interest in the gramophone, and a new contract in 1922 eased his financial problems considerably by fixing his retainer at £500 a year.

At last, in the spring of 1923, he was able to return to Worcestershire to live. Napleton Grange, to the east of the River Severn at Kempsey, five miles to the south of Worcester, is one of the most beautiful of all the houses Elgar rented. Secluded, comfortable

Elgar with his beloved dogs in his garden at Napleton Grange in the twenties.

and roomy without being overpowering (as Severn House had been), he could sit by his piano, the french windows open to the garden, looking at the glorious view of the Malvern Hills rising up across the valley. Here he lived the life of the country gentleman that the public had always assumed him to be. His sisters came to stay, he began to see his old friends, especially Troyte Griffith, again, and he walked and fussed over his dogs. Marco, a spaniel, and Mina, a Cairn, became his inseparable companions, like all happy pets knowing exactly how to extract the maximum sympathy from their master, charging round the garden when he returned home, sitting at the table to keep him company at dinner. On one occasion when Marco was ill, all engagements were cancelled as the distracted Elgar rushed back to the country to be in attendance. The subject of music inevitably came up whenever Willie Reed made one of his frequent visits, but although Elgar would play through chamber music for hours, his own efforts were dismissed with 'Oh, no one wants any more of that nowadays.' Sadly it was beginning to seem true. When he conducted his own works anywhere other than the cities of the Three Choirs, the audiences were small, the reception polite. The concertos held their own, but the oratorios and the First Symphony now seemed hopelessly Edwardian. While the younger composers were grateful for his help (Arthur Bliss, Arnold Bax and Eugene Goossens received special attention) and were aware of his importance, they did not feel comfortable with his music. As Constant Lambert wrote in the thirties, the aggressive Edwardian prosperity that lends so comfortable a background to Elgar's finales is now as strange to us as the England that produced 'Greensleeves' and 'the Woodes so wilde' . . . In consequence much of Elgar's music, through no fault of its own, has for the present generation an almost intolerable air of smugness, self-assurance and autocratic benevolence.

Elgar's music was just old enough to be out-of-date, not yet old enough to be seen in perspective and enjoyed on its own merits. It was suffering from that most twentieth-century phenomenon, the generation gap.

Elgar realised that times had changed and with them the public mood (so did Shaw, who characteristically defended his friend by

George Bernard Shaw (1856-1950), playwright, socialist, music critic and energetic champion of Elgar's music.

attacking the audience in print for having 'the tastes of schoolboys and sporting coster-mongers'). He accepted the situation with the same self-conscious fatalism that he had always professed; music was dead and the struggle had always been useless. He still wanted to write, but the momentum seemed to have gone and Alice was no longer there to force him into the discipline of slogging over the paper. There seemed to be no point in searching through his sketchbooks.

In November 1923 he decided he needed a complete change, not only from music, but from England and everywhere else he had visited. He booked himself onto the 'Hildebrand', a small ship sailing from Liverpool to Madeira, and from there across the South Atlantic to Brazil, its eventual destination being the port of Manaos, over a thousand miles up the Amazon. He had always been fascinated by the sea, whether sailing on it, living by or composing about it, and he did not suffer from sea-sickness, despite a notoriously rough voyage. Perhaps the remedy he was taking for Menière's disease, the complaint of the inner ear from which he suffered, also dispelled the effects of the ocean. The voyage was a great success and he returned after two months at sea full of enthusiasm, especially for the opera houses to be found in nearly every Brazilian town of any size. The depression of the last three years was banished, at least for the time being.

1924 proved to be the busiest year of the decade so far, with recording sessions, conducting engagements and official commissions for composition. These came with his appointment as Master of the King's Musick in May, in succession to Sir Walter Parratt, who had first brought about Elgar's contact with Queen Victoria in 1897. His first duties in the post were to conduct the opening celebrations of the British Empire Exhibition at Wembley Stadium, complete with a huge chorus and the massed bands of the Brigade of Guards. King George V and the Prince of Wales were both due to attend and make speeches. Elgar set himself the task of writing some suitable music for the occasion but the King expressed a determined preference for *Land of Hope and Glory*. New music was not His Majesty's strong point, as he had demonstrated once before when the bandmaster had arranged themes from Strauss's *Elektra* to be played outside Buckingham Palace for the changing of the guard. As they finished, a page approached carrying a message from King George. 'His Majesty does not know what the Band has just played,' it read, 'but it is *never* to be played again.'

Faced with the King's decision the performance of the *Empire March* and *The Pageant of Empire* (eight songs to words by Alfred Noyes) had to wait until later in the Exhibition. It might he thought that Elgar was in his element on such occasions but, while he presented himself as the epitome of regal dignity, he found a false note in much of the ceremonial. At rehearsals he was

overwhelmed by etiquette and red tape . . . everything seems so hopelessly and irredeemably *vulgar* at Court . . . I was standing alone (criticising) in the middle of the enormous stadium . . . 17,000 men, hammering, loudspeakers, amplifiers, four aeroplanes circling over etc. etc. – all mechanical & horrible – no soul & no romance & no imagination.

Earlier in the year The Gramophone Company had embarked on its most ambitious Elgarian project so far; the recording, without cuts and with the minimum of orchestral tampering, of the whole of the Second Symphony. The Royal Albert Hall Orchestra (of which Landon Ronald was the guiding spirit, having

Elgar conducting massed choirs in Land of Hope and Glory at the opening of the British Empire Exhibition at Wembley, 1924. Lt.Col. Adkins of the Royal Military School of Music, Kneller Hall stands behind him. (Radio Times Hulton Picture Lib.)

116

taken it over, in its previous incarnation as the New Symphony Orchestra, when Beecham had walked out in 1908 over the question of deputies) was hired for four sessions. These were spread over two days, 5th and 20th March and for the four movements a total of twenty-seven 'takes' were needed. It was a fine achievement, given all the limitations of acoustical recording. However, within a year this and all other records made in the same way were to be made obsolete by the introduction of the electrical microphone. The microphone had of course been used in radio for some time, but until 1924 it had not been possible to merge the two processes of electronic transmission and reproduction on disc. The development of this technique by Western Electric, as a sideline to their research into telephones, meant that all record companies had not only to abandon all the old methods almost overnight in order to stay in business, they also had to completely re-train their staff from acoustic mechanics to electronic engineers. There was no further studio work for Elgar for the rest of 1924, although one final acoustic session was booked for the following April to complete the first movement, which had not been satisfactory the first time round.

1925 saw the presentation of the Royal Philharmonic Society's Gold Medal, an honour only rarely awarded, and it looked for a time as though the Society might indeed get the Piano Concerto for which they had asked. It seemed also as though Henry Embleton's intensive pleading (on a visit to Paris of the Leeds Choral Union, which Elgar was conducting, the year before) might at last have some effect and win him the third part of the oratorio trilogy that he had wanted for nearly twenty years. But the enthusiasm was soon forgotten and neither project was taken any further. Composition fared badly in the last half of the decade. Between 1925 and 1929 Elgar's complete output consisted of two part-songs, two carols, an arrangement of a motet by Purcell, a Civic Fanfare for the opening of the Hereford Festival of 1927 (of which we possess a 'live' recording of the first performance) and some incidental music for *Beau Brummel* at the Theatre Royal, Birmingham.

He was happier as a local celebrity, motoring around the lanes of his native Worcestershire with Willie Reed, or holding court at each year's Three Choirs Festival, where his interpretations of his own works had become, since the war, almost synonymous with the Festival itself. Although only a few of his best works had in fact been commissioned for the Three Choirs, Elgar was as much associated with it as, in later years, Britten was to be with Aldeburgh. Valued as his wider fame was, Elgar knew that he was most appreciated in his own counties. When he did come to London it was mainly to make records. His reduced activity was

Three Choirs Festival, Gloucester 1923. Elgar has his hand on his brother Frank's shoulder. (Radio Times Hulton Picture Lib.)

Elgar outside the Queen's Hall in the 1920s.

not due to lack of energy, however. After two gruelling days of recording in 1926, (in which he had conducted the *Enigma Variations*, *Cockaigne*, *Pomp and Circumstance Marches 1 & 2*, *Chanson de nuit* and the *Fantasia and Fugue*), he wrote to Schuster:

It is curious that I do not *tire* now – 3 hours solid rehearsal Sunday; – the like Monday & the concert; early on Tuesday 3 hours H.M.V. (large orchestra) Wedy afternoon also Dinner on Tuesday & Theatre last night & I am 69!!

As he reached seventy, Elgar clung still tighter to the few constants in his life; his work for H.M.V., the countryside of the West Midlands and the companionship of his dogs. Friends were dying; Lord Stuart, Sir Sidney Colvin, Sir Herbert Brewer (the Gloucester Cathedral organist) and, greatly missed, Frank Schuster at the end of 1927, who left him £7,000 'for being an English composer worthy to rank with the great masters.'

His popularity was at its lowest ebb and the London concert to mark his birthday was only half full. Manchester was more generous and Adolph Brodsky came out of retirement to play the violin concerto under the composer's direction. To the younger generation and those more conscious of fashion than of merit, he was becoming a museum-piece in his own life-time. Any reference to Elgar to an undergraduate in the twenties was as likely to be greeted with a snigger as with appreciation. Among those to whom it is a tenet of intellectual snobbery to dismiss English music as all sentiment and pastoral idylls, he is still regarded as a purveyor of marches and syrup, even though the symphonies have sometimes recently come not far behind those of Mahler and Beethoven as the most often played in London.

Once again, in 1927, Elgar fell foul of landlords and his request to extend the lease on Napleton Grange was refused. A few months were spent at Battenhall Manor, also on the outskirts of Worcester, but he soon moved to Stratford-on-Avon, where his garden ran down to the river's edge and where he fished from the bank or paddled about in the rowing boat he had bought. There he stayed until the winter of 1929, when, after so many years in rented houses, he at last managed to buy another home. It was the first house he had ever owned in Worcester and Marl Bank was to be his home for the rest of his life.

Among the recordings he made that year were the only examples we have of Elgar as a player. In November 1929 he took it into his head to ask Fred Gaisberg to book the Small Queen's Hall for an extra session the day before he was due to record a number of early pieces for small orchestra. Once installed at the piano he improvised for an hour and, even though he had always professed to

Elgar sits at his piano at
Napleton Grange.

The HMV van sits outside Hereford Cathedral recording Gerontius, 1927.

despise the piano as a means of expression, he found the discipline of improvisation very revealing, especially when he could listen to the results later and extract any material he thought worthwhile. There are five improvisations altogether, each miniature carefully rounded and showing an articulate and natural command of the keyboard.

With the new decade and the final return to Worcester, thoughts of composition were stirring again. He had, in his capacity of Master of the King's Musick, written a short piece in December for Windsor, *A simple carol for His Majesty's happy recovery*; the sort of tribute that had been made for royal events for hundreds of years. For another national institution, the Brass Band, he turned to his beloved River Severn for inspiration, writing a set of four 'pictures' of the valley; *Worcester Castle*, *Tournament*, *Cathedral* and *Commandery*. They were ready for the National Championships to be held at Crystal Palace in September. Bernard Shaw was there and, having sat through the *Severn Suite* rendered by eight different bands, reported back to Elgar (who had dedicated the work to him) with characteristic Shavian directness:

If there is a new edition of the score I think it would be well to drop the old Italian indications and use the language of the bandsmen. For instance. Remember that a minuet is a dance and not a bloody hymn; or steady up for artillery attack; or NOW – like Hell . . .

In the meantime the old sketchbooks were brought out and Elgar set to work completing the last of the *Pomp and Circumstance Marches*, No.5, and dedicated it to George Sinclair's successor as organist at Hereford, Percy Hull. For the oboe a short *Soliloquy* was begun, with Leon Goossens as the intended recipient. But this he did not get as far as orchestrating (the task was eventually taken on by Gordon Jacob and the piece was not finally heard until 1967). His Royal post prompted another suite the following year, but this time it was not the imperial world of marches or ceremony but the nursery, the last in the line of scenes from childhood that already included *Dream Children*, *The Wand of Youth Suites* and *The Starlight Express*. It was prompted by the birth of Princess Margaret to the then Duke and Duchess of York (later George VI and Queen Elizabeth). There is no sign of old age in the seven little movements, except perhaps in the wistfulness of the last (Dreaming-Envoi); the sad, serious and merry dolls are depicted with relish, while No.3, Busy-ness, is innocent and fresh. The themes were from his youth (he had come across some of them while rummaging through a trunk-load of early efforts, dating back as far as 1878), but the orchestration is both mature and shows the lightness of touch which is characteristic of the works of his last years.

The first performance of the *Nursery Suite* was an unusual and private affair. On 23rd May 1931 the press were invited to attend rehearsals and a recording session at Kingsway Hall. The *Nursery Suite* was finished, but the last side was unsatisfactory and a second session had to be arranged. June 4th was fixed and Elgar invited the Duke and Duchess to hear their children's pieces. He also took the opportunity to bring Bernard Shaw and the actors Norman Forbes and Cedric Hardwicke. W.H. Reed, who was then leading the London Symphony Orchestra, remembered:

Upon their arrival Mr. Fred Gaisberg (artistic director of the company) handed them each a copy 'de luxe' of the score, and we then proceeded to play it under Sir Edward's own direction. When we had played the number *The Wagon Passes*, their Royal Highnesses' faces were wreathed in smiles and, at their request, Sir Edward repeated it.

The day before it had been announced that Elgar had been made a Baronet, an elevation of his Knighthood.

Elgar was now working with more vigour and to greater purpose than at any time since the death of his wife. The new spur to composition came at a time when public appreciation of his music, stimulated in celebration of his seventy-fifth birthday, was almost equal to the enthusiasm of before the war. The disinterest of the twenties had, for the time being, been largely dispelled. By November 1931, when he recorded *Falstaff*, H.M.V. had built up a complete catalogue of his major works and the majority of the smaller ones, some of them recorded two or three times since his first studio session in 1914. The vast improvement in gramophone technology meant that anything not made within the previous few years was obsolete. One such was the 1916 recording of the violin concerto. Plans had been made since 1929 to have Kreisler as the soloist in a new version, but he was always too busy or arrived in England when Elgar was unwell. Finally Fred Gaisberg gave up and suggested the fifteen-year-old prodigy Yehudi Menuhin instead, an inspired fusion of youth and old age, proving that Elgar's music did not appeal only to those of his own generation. As well as having a brilliant technique, Menuhin was already an experienced and highly professional musician, but also, as Gaisberg saw, 'a youthful and pliant performer without prejudice, who would respond to his instruction.'

Menuhin was due in London in July and it was arranged that Elgar should go to the Grosvenor House Hotel, where the violinist was staying, to rehearse on the morning of the 12th in preparation for the recording on the following Thursday and Friday. The

Elgar and Yehudi
Menuhin. The famous
photograph taken outside
HMV's Abbey Road
Studios in 1932.

accompanist Ivor Newton, who played for the rehearsal, remembered:

> The boy and the old man took to one another at once . . . Menuhin and Elgar discussed the music like equals, but with great courtesy and lack of self-consciousness on the boy's part. Listening to the discussion, I could not be other than amazed at his maturity of outlook and his ability to raise points without ever sounding like anything but a master violinist discussing a work with a composer for whom he had unbounded respect . . . Most of the time Elgar sat back in a chair with his eyes closed, listening intently, but it was easy to see the impression that Yehudi had made on him . . .

Elgar had heard quite enough by lunchtime to know that he needed to rehearse no more, and departed to Newmarket and the racing. To Bernard Shaw he wrote the next day, 'I am recording the Violin Concerto . . . with Yehudi Menuhin – wonderful boy.' The sessions were something of a triumph and as an interpretation it is still the standard against which all new versions have to be measured. The week afterwards, Elgar wrote to Gaisberg: 'My dear Barbarossa [a nickname in the tradition of Jaeger's 'Mosshead']. I hope our work pleases: we did our best: of course *Yehudi* is wonderful & will be splendid – I fear the composer will not be up to . . . standard.'

In the way of performance, Elgar's music abounded that year. At Sadler's Wells Ninette de Valois choreographed the *Nursery Suite* with Constant Lambert (who had earlier been the hero of the generation most alienated from Elgar) conducting. The Three Choirs Festival was held at Worcester for the last time in Elgar's lifetime, and it was almost entirely devoted to his works. There were performances of the *First Symphony*, *Gerontius*, *For the Fallen*, *The Music Makers*, the *Piano Quintet* and the first hearing of the orchestral arrangement of the *Severn Suite*. Despite occasional bouts of sciatica and lumbago, he was in excellent form and well able to play his part in the B.B.C.'s Elgar Festival in December, mounted partly in answer to fierce criticism by Sir Landon Ronald that the corporation was ignoring him. Amends were soon made when the B.B.C. announced that it had commissioned a new Symphony.

Almost as much debate and controversy surrounds the sketches for a Third Symphony as *The Enigma Variations*, mainly because its origins and its state of completion at the composer's death are sufficiently vague to invite speculation. It does seem certain that the initial prompting for a symphony came from Bernard Shaw, who wrote from an Atlantic cruise in January 1932, 'Why don't you make the B.B.C. order a new symphony? It can afford it.' Shaw referred to the idea again on a postcard in June, and there is obviously a serious suggestion behind the humour: 'Why not a Financial Symphony? Allegro: Impending Disaster. Lento Mesto: Stony Broke. Scherzo: Light Heart and Empty Pocket. All° con brio: Clouds Clearing.'

More for convenience than anything else, since it also included the address to which records of the *Severn Suite* should be sent, Elgar passed this postcard to Fred Gaisberg, adding in the covering letter, 'perhaps H.M.V. would like to commission (say £5,000) for such a symphony as *G.B.S.* suggests: the p.c. is worth more than my music!' Gaisberg showed both to colleagues and, possibly, to Sir Landon Ronald, who was on the Governing body of the B.B.C. as well as being an advisor to the Gramophone Company. Ronald did not actually moot the subject with Elgar until November 11th, when he wrote to Shaw thanking him for proposing the plan. However, by that stage it seems that his intention to write another symphony was not one of the best-kept secrets in the musical world. Rosa Burley alleged that, at a tea-party at the Worcester Festival, he had said 'that since no one wanted his music nowadays it was useless for him to complete the score of his Third Symphony although it was actually written.' In fact it was a long way short of completion and it is doubtful whether, at that point, he had any clear idea of the main themes.

However, he accepted the commission and set about assembling his material as usual, working from one fragment to another, inserting a passage in one movement then switching back to fit a scrap into another. Gradually through 1933, the segments began to have an order and, as he had during the writing of the violin concerto and the chamber music, Willie Reed was often on hand to try over the themes while Elgar filled in the harmonic basis on the piano. As many as twenty or thirty bars together were clearly complete on paper, whether in short score or just a single line of melody, but only six pages of the first movement emerged in full score. Like Mozart, it was plain that the shape of work was finished in his head and just needed the physical effort to write it down. He told Reed,

it was not going to be cast in the same form as the two earlier symphonies, but was going to be simpler in construction and design. He was going to revert to the old-fashioned repeat in the exposition of the first movement with a *prima* and *seconda volta*. The second movement was to be of a light character with contrasts, but not quick: it was to be a slow-moving kind of Scherzo. Of the slow movement he wrote out the main themes on a single stave for me to play them on the violin . . . The last movement was to be fiery and rugged; but I never could find out how it was to end. Whenever I asked the question he always became mysterious and vague, and said, 'Ah, that we shall see,' or something non-committal; and I could not induce him to begin the slow movement at the beginning.

AYOT ST LAWRENCE, WELWYN, HERTS
STATION: WHEATHAMPSTEAD, L.& N.E.R. 2¼ MILES.
TELEGRAMS: BERNARD SHAW, CODICOTE.
TELEPHONE: CODICOTE 18. 29th June 1932

The above address is right for the suite. Send it to Charlotte: suites to the suite.

I have had only just had my gramophone fixed up to my wireless. My first try on it will be Falstaff.

We go to Malvern on the 24th. I am neurotic with overwork.

Why not a Financial Symphony? Allegro: Impending Disaster. Lento mesto: Stony Broke. Scherzo: Light Heart and Empty Pocket. All° con brio: Clouds Clearing.

G.B.S.

a

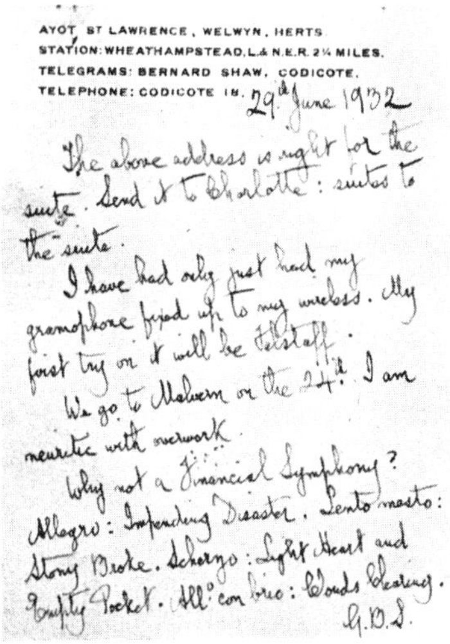

a. The post-card from Shaw to Elgar that started the process for the commissioning of the Third Symphony. For convenience Elgar sent it with a covering letter to Gaisberg.

b-c. The covering letter – tongue in cheek but hopefully suggesting a composition fee of £5,000.

d. Gaisberg asked whether he could keep G.B.S's post-card. Elgar (and his dog Marco) agreed.

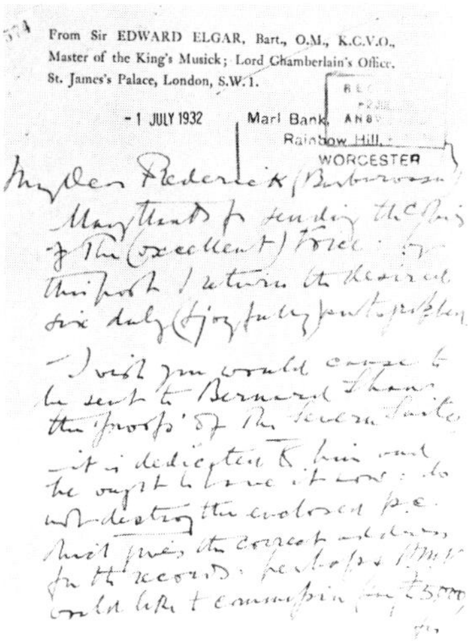

From Sir EDWARD ELGAR, Bart., O.M., K.C.V.O.,
Master of the King's Musick; Lord Chamberlain's Office,
St. James's Palace, London, S.W.1.

-1 JULY 1932 Marl Bank, Rainbow Hill, WORCESTER

My dear Frederick (Barbarossa)

Many thanks for sending the copies of the (excellent) voice: by this post I return the desired ...

I wish you would cause to be sent to Bernard Shaw the proofs of the Severn Suite — it is dedicated to him and he ought to have it now: do not destroy the enclosed p.c. which gives the correct address for the record: perhaps HMV would like to commission for £5000

b

and a symphony as G.B.S. suggests: the p.c. is worth more than my music!

I love to ...

Edward Elgar

Address the suite to Mrs Bernard Shaw, Ayot St Lawrence, Welwyn, Herts

c

MARL BANK,
RAINBOW HILL,
WORCESTER.

Telephone: Worcester, 934. Telegraph: Elgar, Worcester.

RECEIVED 7 JUL 1932 ANSWERED

This is to certify that Frederick Barbarossa, as a reward for general good conduct, may hold as his own property in perpetuity the post-card in the writing of G. B. S. addressed to the under-signed adumbrating the manufacture of a symphony.

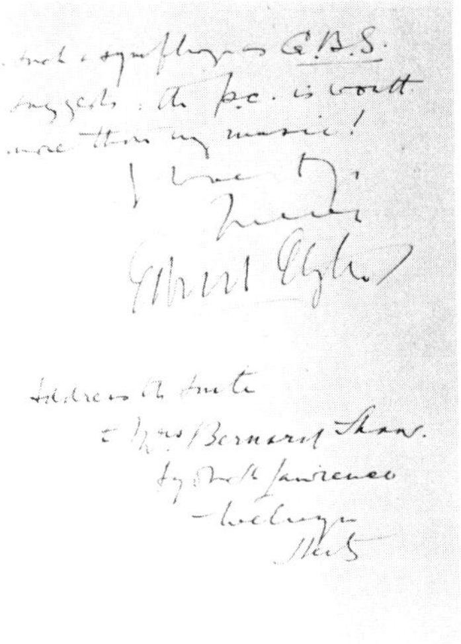

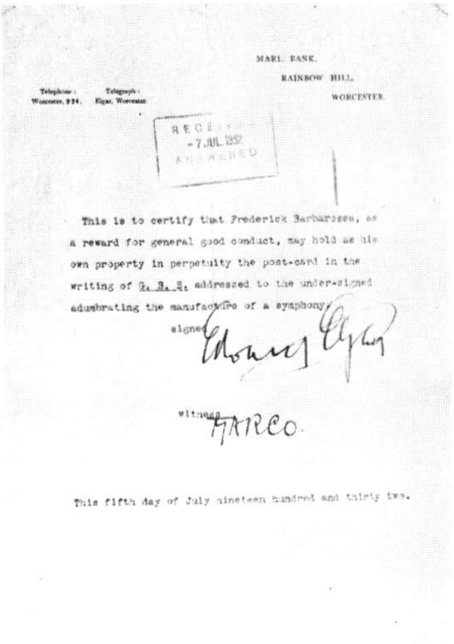

signed Edward Elgar

witness MARCO

This fifth day of July nineteen hundred and thirty two.

d

e-f. By April 1933 the symphony was clearly sketched in his mind although he was still not sure of the order of the middle two movements. However he was confident that all would be finished within a year. Was the 'bad turn' the beginning of his fatal illness?

From Sir EDWARD ELGAR, Bart., O.M., K.C.V.O.,
Master of the King's Musick; Lord Chamberlain's Office,
St. James's Palace, London, S.W.1.

27 APR 1933

Dear Willie:

I like your idea to announce the symphony for the Norwich Festival of 1934: that will give us all full time for preparation in all departments, proofs, rehearsals, etc. So if you like to proceed pray do so: you do not worry me!! So if there is anything else to ask or answer be sure to write.

I had a sudden bad turn two days ago — but am getting all right again.

Kind regards
Yours ever
Edward Elgar PTO

e

Symphony in C minor.

I. Allegro
II. Allegretto
III. Adagio
IV. Allegro

Now the trouble is that I have not decided finally the positions of II & III

Stamped by 3

f

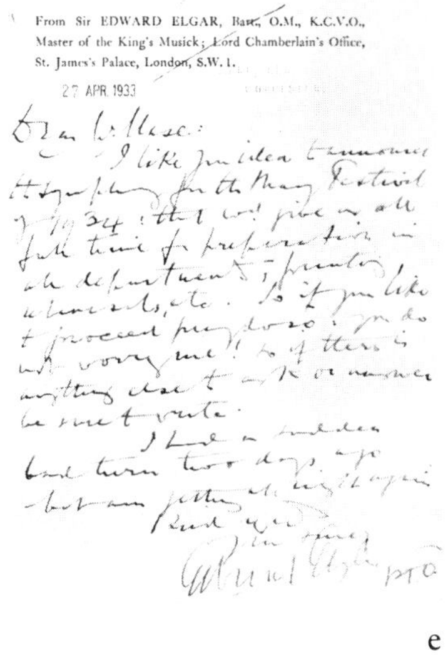

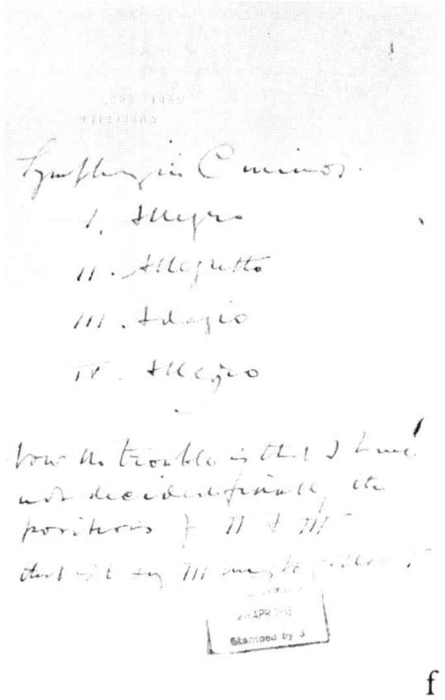

August 1932, George Bernard Shaw's garden party at Malvern. (Radio Times Hulton Picture Library.)

He would perhaps have progressed considerably faster had the symphony been the only project on his mind – he usually completed a work more or less within a year of the start of concentrated thought – but he was determined to complete an opera at the same time. He had been contemplating the idea for most of the century, and both Richter and Strauss had pressed him for one. In 1914 he had thought of something by Thomas Hardy as a possible subject, and later he asked Shaw for an original libretto. Shaw declined on the basis that his words had a music of their own and could not be set satisfactorily to notes. Eventually Elgar, still wanting an English text, fell back on his deep knowledge of Jacobean literature, turning not to Shakespeare (as he had for *Falstaff* and as he had planned for a setting of 'King Lear') but to Ben Jonson's 'The Devil is an Ass', the last of his great comedies, written in 1616 two years after 'Bartholomew Fair'.

To produce a coherent operatic libretto from this he approached Sir Barry Jackson, himself an accomplished playwright and founder of Birmingham Repertory Theatre and the Malvern Festival, with which Shaw was strongly associated. In a letter to Reed after Elgar's death, Jackson said:

The opening of EMI's Abbey Road Studios on 12th November 1931. Elgar conducts, W. H. Reed leads the London Symphony Orchestra. On the steps sit Sir Walford Davies (hidden by the banister), Sir Landon Ronald and Shaw. (EMI).

it was no surprise to hear that his inclination ran in the direction of that full blooded dramatist Ben Jonson. What did surprise me was that, instead of taking one of the better known plays, he had set his heart upon . . . a work which always appeared to me quite moribund . . . A fortnight later . . . diving through the voluminous spate of words and incidents, I found at the bottom what seemed to be a splendid story for an opera, which proved that Sir Edward was right from the first . . . The story was fined down to the uttermost dramatic limits in my version; but Sir Edward was determined that the work should be on a grandiose scale; for he added that, if he ever composed an opera it was going to be a grand opera. Amongst his music were numberless sheets of MS. with a large B.J. in the corner. It would have been just like him to honour me by asking my assistance, rather than someone better equipped, simply because of the similarity of the initials.

Elgar's enthusiasm for the stage carried over into every detail of the project. Stage plans were drawn, with Elgar even marking in the props and the positions of the characters, a duty rather outside the normal concerns of the composer. The title was to be *The Spanish Lady* (though Elgar never went to Spain he often pictured it musically) and while the plot remained within the confines

Letter to Gaisberg
asking him to travel with
Elgar to Paris. It was to be
Elgar's first trip by
aeroplane and he recalls
his visit with his brother
in law in 1880.

of 'The Devil is an Ass', the actual dialogue came from many Jonsonian sources, including extracts from the masques to provide suitably lyrical interludes. Elgar knew exactly what he wanted; he wrote to Jackson in September 1932,

. . . the chorus might be *plausibly* introduced for any effect of movement – not as you will feel – static. A small chorus – not a huge crowd. The period dresses appeal to me for opera &, padded out as you cd, do it, might make a *warm & full* thing. I do not see any real fault with characters pairing off as you feel they will do. Meecraft (good bass) Dotterel (Beckmesser Baritone) appeal to me to characterise musically.

By January the music was progressing well; 'It quite cheered me . . .', he told Jackson on 23rd, 'to know you liked my new tunes – a little anyway. I feel somewhat shy of writing at my age but on listening to it I fail to notice any marked senility.' For many ideas he ransacked his old sketch-books; discarded recitatives from *The Kingdom*, 39 bars of his *Pas Redoublé* march of 1882, a song originally called *April*, a passage once bound for the *Crown of India*, even music from the days of wind quintets on Sunday afternoons in the potting-shed almost sixty years before: these were all re-drafted and fitted into the scheme. In all there are 180 fragments, some running to as much as ten pages, and although there is not enough material to reconstruct the opera completely or to simulate the final orchestration there is enough, as Dr. Percy Young has successfully proved, to prepare a suite of dances for string orchestra from the sections left in short score. They show not only that in his late seventies Elgar was still creatively fertile but also that he had retained his lightness of touch and had found a new economy of expression. The orchestrating of the Bach *Fantasia and Fugue* and the Handel 'Overture' were preliminary indications of his growing interest in pre-romantic forms, showing, I believe, that he was not impervious – as his contemporaries thought – to new trends in style or to the exploration of neo-classicism. It is, perhaps, possible that the long period of inactivity was as much due to a crisis of style – the late romantic trying, within his own highly individual idiom, to find an apt language for the twentieth-century – as to personal griefs. Elgar was a conservative, and it was not easy for him to admit the need for change. He could not throw over the assumptions of the need for melody and tonality as Schönberg had done, yet he knew that after the First World War the needs of audiences were different, hence his often repeated assertion that no one wanted his music anymore. *The Nursery Suite*, the ballad-opera form of *The Spanish Lady* indicate that he was at least partly beginning to reconcile himself with the attitudes of his English juniors.

Elgar departing on his first flight from Croydon Aerodrome, 1933.

Work was interrupted in May 1933 by a visit to France, his last trip abroad. In Paris he conducted Menuhin in the Violin Concerto; the great Rumanian musician Georges Enesco taking the preliminary rehearsals. 'Enesco rehearsed the orchestra superbly,' Menuhin has written, 'comprehending the work so well that when Elgar came over for the performance he took us through it without once stopping. The French received it politely, but it has never been performed in Paris since.' For the first time in his life Elgar flew by aeroplane, an experience that he found exhilarating. Fred Gaisberg accompanied him, 'It was a fine day and Elgar enjoyed it with just a twinge of anxiety as he would grip the rails when we struck some air pockets on his first flight. He seemed to feel like a hero and had a daring smile on his face like a pleased boy.' The next day, after lunch with the Menuhin family, Gaisberg and Elgar set out to visit the ailing Delius who lived at Grez-sur-Loing just outside Fontainebleau. 'Delius was sitting in the middle of the room, facing the windows, very upright, with his hands resting on the arms of a big rolling chair. Illuminated by the afternoon sun, his face looked long and pale and rather immobile . . . his speech, halting at first, became more fluent as he warmed up to his subject and we forgot his impediment of speech. He seemed mentally alert . . . I gleaned that they were both non-keyboard composers, both had important compositions under way. Both emphasised the importance of the gramophone to them and Delius also stressed the wireless . . .' They talked about flying and Elgar told his colleague, 'The rising from the ground was a little difficult; you cannot tell exactly how you are going to stand it. When once you have reached the heights it is very different. There is a delightful feeling of elation in sailing through gold and silver clouds. It is, Delius, rather like your music – a little intangible sometimes, but always very beautiful. I should have liked to stay there for ever.' Delius was impressed, as Gaisberg remembered, 'In a lordly way he waved his left arm to instruct Mrs. Delius: "Dear, we must fly the next time we go to England," ' Champagne was brought and toasts were drunk.

The celebrations continued after the flight home, when they were met on the runway at Croydon Aerodrome by Carice and Billy Reed with a bottle of wine to toast his birthday, his decoration from the President of France (awarded when he went as guest of honour to a state function at the Artillery School), and the addition of the Grand Cross of the Victorian Order to his collection of British achievements. When he arrived home at Marl Bank in the heat of that summer, he was met by suitably welcoming enthusiasm from his dogs and he wrote a small orchestral piece and called it *Mina* in their honour. It was his last completed work.

In the world outside, there were once again signs of alarm. For the second time during his life Elgar found himself disillusioned with the activities of Germany. 'I am in a maze regarding events in Germany,' he wrote to Frank Schuster's sister Adela, 'what are they doing? In this morning's paper it is said that the great conductor Bruno Walter &, stranger still, Einstein, are ostracised: are we all mad? The Jews have always been my best and kindest friends – the pain of this news is unbearable and I do not know what it really means.'

In the meantime, when he was not too exhausted by the heat to work, he continued to look at the third symphony and at the opera. On August 17th he went to London to conduct the Second Symphony and to talk about a forthcoming recording of the Piano Quintet with Harriet Cohen and the Stratton Quartet. That evening he talked to Adrian Boult about the new symphony, and it was decided that it would be a good idea to record the work with the B.B.C. Symphony Orchestra early so that it could be released two or three days before the first performance. It would seem that the work was far enough advanced at this stage for Elgar to be confident that he was within sight of finishing it. This impression is supported by the fact that ten days later he took his portfolio (which he kept by his bedside) and played it through after tea to Fred Gaisberg, Scott Sunderland and Sir Barry Jackson. Gaisberg described it in his diary:

The opening – a great broad burst *animato* gradually resolving into a fine broad melody for strings. This is fine. 2nd movement is slow & tender in true Elgar form. The 3rd movement is an ingenious Scherzo, well designed: a delicate, feathery short section of 32nds contrasted with a moderate sober section. 4th movement is a spirited tempo with full resources, developed at some length. The whole work strikes me as youthful and fresh – 100% Elgar without a trace of decay. The work is complete as far as structure & design and scoring is well advanced. In his own mind he is enthusiastically satisfied with it and says it is his best work.

Whether he was playing only from scraps that we now possess, whether there were amongst his papers portions that were not found after his death or whether he was in fact only improvising from such material as was at hand, it is now impossible to establish. Consequently, because anything that cannot be proven is a candidate for a mystery, speculation still rumbles occasionally about how finished the score actually was – some writers even suggesting that somewhere in the nether regions of the B.B.C. a full score is hidden. Sadly, this seems an imaginative but inconclusive dream, and the Third Symphony can be said to have had its first and only performance in Elgar's music room that August afternoon.

The following week the Three Choirs Festival started at Hereford. Elgar stayed in the Priory and spent much of the time sitting in the garden. Every day he held a tea party and one day Shaw, appearing from the Cathedral performance of *Elijah*, rashly announced that the trouble with Mendelssohn was that he could not orchestrate. That was too much for Elgar, who promptly took the full score on his knees and took Shaw through it, bar by bar. That evening he conducted *The Dream of Gerontius* for the last time.

After the festival his sciatica returned and he was in great pain. It was decided that he should undergo an exploratory operation and in the first week in October he went into South Bank Nursing Home in Worcester, just along from the house he had shared with his sister Lucy in the Bath Road in 1883. The operation found that his condition was far more serious than had been thought. He had a malignant tumour pressing on the sciatic nerve. Elgar was dying of cancer and could live for a year at the most. He was not told, however, and only Carice and W.H. Reed were allowed to know. At the end of November he lapsed into a coma and was given the last rites. However, surprisingly he recovered and by December

In December 1933 Gaisberg took the photographer Fred Hempstead to South Bank Nursing Home Worcester at Elgar's request.

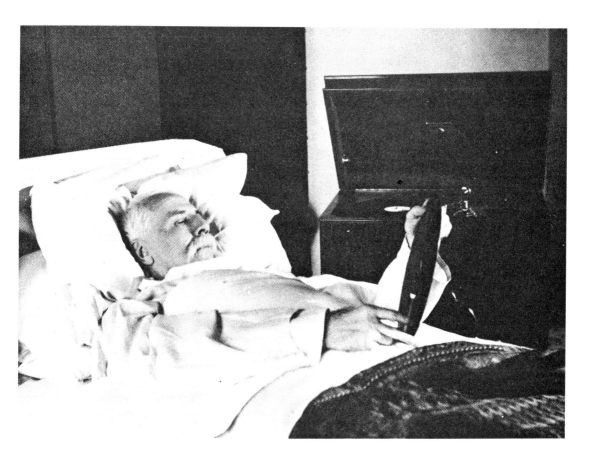

Dear Mr Gaisberg,
    I had the opportunity of playing the Mina record to father today. He wants me to tell you that he much enjoyed hearing it – & thinks it is kind of you to have had it done. He hopes you will not mind his saying that it is too fast. He knows the time was not marked – it wants more stress on the first part. The next time should be much softer *perhaps* –

Later on the part played by Billie Reed (sic) is twice as fast as it should be – & the loud part (the first note of the 2nd time) does not come out enough.

He is so tired & make all these criticisms – & hopes you may have an opportunity of making another record – he does not wish this one published as it stands.
    Yours *........*
        Carice S. Blake.

Carice's letter to Gaisberg giving criticisms from her father of the record of 'Mina'. Elgar died a week later.

he was allowed to see friends, deal with his own correspondence and organise Gaisberg to visit him with a photographer. He was too ill to work but he listened to the gramophone for as much of the day as he could; the new records of the quintet giving him more pleasure than anything, perhaps because it was so associated with his wife's last days.

Early in January he was allowed to go home to Marl Bank but he gradually declined. To keep his spirits up, however, Gaisberg conceived an elaborate plan to make one more record, connecting Elgar to the studio in London by means of a microphone and loudspeaker attached to a Post Office land line. In this way he could supervise the whole process from his sick-bed. The old composer was delighted and when, on January 22nd, Gaisberg arrived at Marl Bank, he found (after an afternoon nap) Elgar impatient and excited. Sir Ivor Atkins, Troyte Griffith, Madeline Grafton (his niece), his secretary Miss Clifford, his valet Richard Mountford and all the household were summoned. In Studio No.1 at Abbey Road W.H. Reed was standing by with the London Symphony Orchestra conducted by Lawrence Collingwood. Elgar thanked the orchestra for their three cheers and then started rehearsing them for the record of the triumphal march from *Caractacus*. At the end he insisted on hearing the *Woodland Interlude* twice. The maid dutifully tried to leave to make the tea. 'This is much more important', he told her, 'than getting tea ready.'

The following Sunday Reed and Gaisberg came down to see him for the last time, and took him the hastily-made records. In return he gave them the score of *Mina* which they duly recorded and sent to him. On February 15th he was well enough to listen and dictate criticisms of it to Carice but it was plain that he was almost at the end of his strength. At a quarter to eight in the morning, on 23rd February 1934 Elgar died, aged seventy-six. It was a sad year, for within a few months English music also lost Delius and Holst.

He had wanted, at one time, to be buried where the Teme meets the River Severn, but in the event he lies in the plot Troyte Griffith had found for him, next to Alice in the graveyard of St. Wulstan's, Little Malvern. Three days later only a few friends attended the funeral on a fine day when the snow lay on the hillside around the church, and no flowers or music adorned the service. But later, in the Cathedral, the full forces of Worcester and the London Symphony Orchestra justly remembered him.

How great a composer was Elgar? It is a question Englishmen have been asking themselves rather self-consciously for the last fifty years or more. He undoubtedly wrote masterpieces: *The Dream of Gerontius*, *The Kingdom*, *The Enigma Variations*, *Introduction and Allegro*, the two Symphonies and the concertos are as fine as anything written in Britain. Elgar's music has, moreover, a far wider appeal. Alone amongst English composers between Purcell and Britten, his music is exportable. As Constant Lambert wrote, it 'is as national in its way as the music of Vaughan Williams but, by using material that in type can be related back to the nineteenth-century German composers, Elgar avoids any suspicion of provincial dialect.' His music is accessible, beautifully constructed and never afraid of exploiting melody, but not at the expense of clarity or emotional depth. As an orchestrator he has few equals, for he was involved in and loved orchestras all his life. Writing in 1920 George Bernard Shaw said,

Elgar, neither an imitator nor a voluptuary, went his own way without bothering to invent a new language, and by sheer personal originality produced symphonies that are really symphonies in the Beethovenian sense . . . neither I nor any living man can say with certainty whether these . . . are the stigmata of what we call immortality. But they look to me very like it.

In the end all music needs only one justification. Does it *move* the listener. Any amount diverts, entertains and does not repel, but unless it reaches deeper, it is not great. The Christmas before Elgar died, he received a letter from T.E. Lawrence. 'Dear Sir Edward,' he wrote, 'This is from my cottage and we have just been playing your 2nd Symphony . . . We agreed that you must be written to and told (if you are well enough to be bothered) that this symphony gets further under our skins than anything else in the record library at Clouds Hill . . . Generally we play the Symphony last of all, towards the middle of the night, because nothing comes off very well after it. One seems to stop there.'

Elgar at the Three Choirs Festival, 1932.

Bibliography

Edward Elgar. *Letters to Nimrod*. ed. Percy M. Young. Dobson Books, London 1965.

Edward Elgar. *A Future for English Music* and other lectures. ed. Percy M. Young. Dobson Books, London 1968.

Edward Elgar. *My Friends Pictured Within*. Novello & Co. London.

Percy M. Young. *Elgar O.M.* Revised ed. White Lion, London 1973.

Michael Kennedy. *Portrait of Elgar*. Oxford University Press 1968.

R.J. Buckley. *Sir Edward Elgar*. London 1904.

Basil Maine. *Elgar: His Life and Works*. London 1933.

Jerrold Northrop Moore. *Elgar: A Life in Photographs*. Oxford Univ. Press. 1972.

Jerrold Northrop Moore. *Elgar on Record*. Oxford University Press 1974.

W.H. Reed. *Elgar as I Knew Him*. Gollancz. 1973.

Ian Parrott. *Elgar*. J.M. Dent & Sons. London 1971.

Rosa Burley & Frank C. Carruthers. *Edward Elgar: The Record of a Friendship*. Barrie & Jenkins. London 1972.

Mrs. Richard Powell. *Edward Elgar: Memories of a Variation*. Methuen 1947.

Percy M. Young. *Alice Elgar: Portrait of a Victorian Lady*. Dobson Books 1978.

Hubert Leicester. *Forgotten Worcester*. Worcester 1932.

Sir Henry Wood. *My Life of Music*. Gollancz. 1938.

Sir Adrian Boult. *My Own Trumpet*. Hamish Hamilton. London. 1973.

Ivor Newton. *At The Piano*. Hamish Hamilton. London.

Yehudi Menuhin. *Unfinished Journey*. Macdonald & Jane's. London 1977.

Sir Arnold Bax. *Farewell My Youth*. Longmans. London 1943.

Constant Lambert. *Music Ho*. Faber & Faber. London 1934.

Index

Selected listing of references

Illustrations are indicated in bold type

136

137